TREE ADVENTURES AT TAHOE

Rob Haulenbeek

TREE ADVENTURES

AT TAHOE

by Rod Haulenbeek

Wide-(eye)d Publications
P. O. Box 964
Carnelian Bay, CA 96140

This book is dedicated to Lovers: Adventure Lovers, Armchair Adventure Lovers, Tahoe Lovers, and just plain Tree Lovers

ISBN: 1-885155-03-4

Printed and bound in the United States of America.

Printing Information   1 2 3 4 5 6 7 8 9 10

TABLE OF CONTENTS

On the Cover: This cartoon depicts the problem of the true Tree Lover: not being able to see the Lake for the Trees.

HOW TO USE THIS BOOK

This section will help you plan your Tree Adventures, because there are many options in this book. This book has three kinds of Tree Adventures in it. Adventure 1 is an Adventure in Appreciation of what amazing organisms trees are. Adventures 2 through 7 are Adventures in Identification of 16 kinds of trees and 23 kinds of shrubs found at Tahoe, through examples with exact locations. Adventures 7 and 8 are Adventures in Magnificence, a search for beautiful old trees.

Adventure 1 introduces you to the two main kinds of trees at Tahoe, and it gives some principles about these trees which will be useful in later Adventures. Time required: 1 to 2 hours.

Adventures 2, 3 and 4 are segments of a trip around Lake Tahoe at Lake elevation, introducing you to one to three species at a time. These Adventures have road logs and proceed clockwise because that is a better direction to go (but if your plans indicate going the other direction it's still a good trip). Time required: 1 to 2 hours for each Adventure.

Adventure 5 takes you both higher and lower than Lake level, from 8900 feet on Mount Rose Summit to 4500 feet at Reno. There you will encounter different kinds of trees and shrubs than found at Lakeside. Time required: A full day.

Adventure 6 is an exploration of Idlewild Park in Reno, a city with three arboreta. Idlewild Park has many beautiful landscaped non-native trees in a lake setting. This Adventure can be a spinoff of Adventure 5. Time required: 2 to 3 hours.

Adventure 7 is a hike to Vikingshom Castle, on a lush mountainside with trees and shrubs native of Tahoe but easily seen on this lovely hike. Time required: 3 to 4 hours.

Adventure 8 is for people who love to look at magnificent stands of trees in old-growth forests. These trees are easily accessible by vehicle. Time required: 4 to 6 hours.

Adventure 9 is for people who, like me, want to see the largest and most magnificent specimens of a particular species. Time required: 4 to 6 hours.

Adventure 10 is for people who want to know what to see any month of the year. Since you already know where different kinds of trees are, you can check out how they look whenever you visit. Time required: 1 year!

There are also seven Appendices. Appendix B has three Side Trips for people wanting to see something different: Side Trip A explores the U.S.F.S. Visitor Center and Tallac Historic Site on the South Shore. This area has an arboretum, several historic buildings, an area where you can look at large beautiful fish through a window, and even trees gnawed by beavers! Side Trip B is a short visit to the home of the Washoe Pine, and is for people who want to see rare trees. Side Trip C visits the historic and starkly beautiful Donner Pass area.

The other Appendices give relevant information about both Tahoe and Trees which is available but difficult to find; this information is gathered here for reference. Appendix A gives an idea of the size and character of each of the communities at Tahoe. Appendix C gives the Latin names for all plants mentioned in this book, because common names are not always precise. Appendix D is geared to help you identify the trees and shrubs you are most likely to find at Tahoe. Appendix E is a listing of mountain peaks which define the Lake Tahoe and Truckee River Basins. Appendix F gives the rather amazing dimensions of a typical old-age Jeffrey Pine tree in the Tahoe forest. Appendix G gives information about the water in Lake Tahoe.

Many of the people who come to Tahoe are repeat visitors; this book was designed so that they can take one or more Adventures this trip, and some more on the next trip. Also, the Adventures are almost independent, so you don't need to go in any particular order; although it will help you to go through the first five Adventures first. I have included Treasure Maps with some of the Adventures, because you will be seeking true Treasures.

FOREWORD

There is a lake on the Utah-Idaho border similar to Lake Tahoe: the same size, shape and elevation, the mountains surrounding it are similar in size to Lake Tahoe's. But Bear Lake's sparse trees are small and stunted, and one look at that lake tells me what makes Lake Tahoe special: its beautiful forest.

At Tahoe trees extend into the heavens, lush, straight and unyielding. They are not as tall as those in the rain forests of the Pacific Northwest, but it is not always damp and rainy here either. Other forests have a greater species diversity, but the 39 native tree and shrub species described in this book are just about the right number for us Tree Lovers — enough to be interesting but not enough to overwhelm us with minute differences.

The trees could hardly have picked a better place to grow: there is plenty of sunsine, plenty of water falling from the heavens, and temperatures warmer than those at Bear Lake. And in the middle of it all is a gem of a lake, Tahoe.

Though not the best in any category of lakes, it is very good in many categories. The eleventh deepest lake in the world, it certainly is not the biggest (although it is as large as the total of the four largest United States man-made lakes). Lake Tahoe is billed as having the third clearest water of any lake in the world. Crater Lake in Oregon has clearer water, but it could fit in one corner of Lake Tahoe.

Most of the large lakes in the world have been overpopulated, hiding their natural beauty. Not so with Lake Tahoe: there are communities here, but only on the South Shore does one feel like a suburbanite; and there are stretches of highway with no signs of civilization in sight.

This book is the celebration of the beauty of Lake Tahoe and what happens when Man coexists peaceably with Nature. It is divided into a number of Tree Adventures, suitable for travel by people in vehicles, on foot, or even in armchairs. The area covered by each Adventure is different, because different aspects of the Trees can be best covered this way.

Strictly speaking, the Lake Tahoe Basin is the Lake itself and its drainage basin, an area which cannot by itself express the soul of Tahoe. Any book about this area has to include the Truckee River Basin downstream from the Lake, because these areas are soulmates (see Appendix E for a map of these basins and a table of some of the mountain peaks that define them).

The map below shows the locations of the Tree Adventures. Good luck and Happy Tree Hunting!

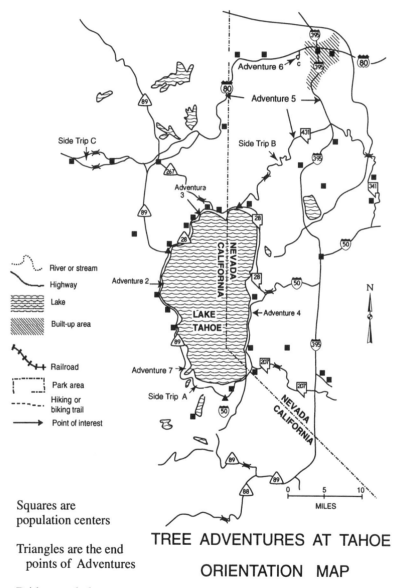

Squares are
  population centers

Triangles are the end
  points of Adventures

Bridge symbols are
  mountain passes

TREE ADVENTURES AT TAHOE

ORIENTATION MAP

THANKS TO...

Many, many librarians for helping me find relevant literature.

Jim Ross for helping me explore Idlewild Park.

Miriam Biro for helping me with Tahoe City history and in my search for Magnificent Trees.

Gay Eitel and Mac Magary for information about the U.S.F. S. Visitor Center and the Tallac Historic Site.

Faye Andersen of Sierra Pacific Power for information about the hydroelectric plants.

Pat Watson for help with map generation.

Dick Haulenbeek for editing help.

Gene Haulenbeek for the cover cartoon.

Jeanne for helping me road-test the Adventures.

ADVENTURE 1

The Two Main Trees at Tahoe Lakeside

In this Adventure, while examining two common Lake Tahoe tree species, you will find out many fascinating things about trees. You may start anywhere at Lake level except on creek banks and beaches.

Almost certainly there are two different species of conifer trees within 100 feet of you. The first species has six-inch needles in numerous bundles of three radiating from branches, cones which are either horizontal or hanging, and plentiful six-inch fat and pointed cones on the ground under larger trees. This is **Jeffrey Pine**. The second species has one-inch needles all along horizontal branches, no cones under large trees, and upright cones limited to the top third of larger trees. This tree is **White Fir**. Together the two species make up about 95 percent of the trees at Lake level.

When I see two trees dominating an area, I ask why. The answer has two parts, climate and history.

Lake Tahoe Climate

Lake Tahoe climate can best be explained by looking at what happens through the year. In winter, water-saturated air comes from the Pacific Ocean. As the air crosses the Sierra Nevada, pressure decreases and the air, a gas, cools. As it cools, the amount of water vapor air can hold decreases; the excess precipitates from the atmosphere as either rain or snow.

Lake Tahoe is at an elevation of about 6200 feet and a latitude of about 39 degrees; in winter daily temperature varies from a high in the 30s or 40s to a low in the 10s or 20s. This means that the precipitation usually falls as snow, and that temperatures are much warmer than they are in the Rocky Mountains hundreds of miles to the east. The proper air temperature is important for snowfall — Lake Tahoe gets much more snow than Antarctica, because air temperature is so cold there that air can hold very little moisture. Geographers consider Antarctica a desert!

Wintertime fronts bring storm after storm into this area; the result is prodigious amounts of snow, an average of almost 20 feet yearly at Lake level. Between storms, there are many sunny days here (about 75 prcent of winter days here have some sunshine). Most of the melting snow evaporates or sinks into the snow; there is little runoff. This means that the moisture that falls stays in the area. Snow cover insulates the ground from very cold temperatures, and keeps trees from dehydrating during winter.

Spring brings average high temperatures in the 40s to 60s and average low temperatures in the 20s or 30s, good temperatures for tree growth. Some water from melting snow sinks into the ground, providing moisture for tree growth.

Summer here has mild temperatures — average highs in the 60s to 80s and average lows in the 30s or 40s; but the air is very dry (relative humidity of less than 20 percent is not uncommon). A stationary high pressure area in the Pacific Ocean keeps clouds from entering Tahoe in summer, so there is essentially no precipitation — only about 3 percent of average annual precipitation falls during summer. Trees need to be drought-resistant to survive Tahoe summers.

In fall, average high temperature is in the 40s to 70s and average low temperature is in the 20s or 30s. There is more rain and snow than in summer, but not usually enough to support tree growth; trees have to withstand insufficient moisture until the snows start in November.

The overall Tahoe weather pattern is thus mild snowy winters; moist cool springs; dry warm summers; and dry mild falls. Trees best adapted to such conditions thrive here.

Within these overall conditions temperature and precipitation vary. The schematic cross section on the next page shows how these conditions change from place to place. At the Sierra Nevada Crest six miles west of Tahoe City, average temperatures are lower; a good rule of thumb is that temperature decreases two degrees for each 1000 feet of elevation gain. Annual precipitation here is about 60 inches. At Tahoe City, on the west shore of the Lake, annual precipitation is about 31 inches.

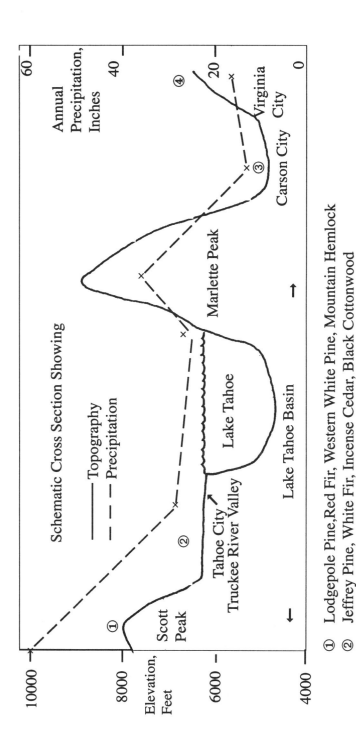

Schematic Cross Section Showing

— Topography
--- Precipitation

Annual Precipitation, Inches

Elevation, Feet

Scott Peak

Tahoe City
Truckee River Valley

Lake Tahoe

Lake Tahoe Basin

Marlette Peak

Carson City

Virginia City

① Lodgepole Pine, Red Fir, Western White Pine, Mountain Hemlock

② Jeffrey Pine, White Fir, Incense Cedar, Black Cottonwood

③ Fremont Cottonwood

④ Single-leaf Pinyon Pine, Utah Juniper

As water preciptates from the sky, there is less water vapor available, so there is usually less precipitation as one heads east.

The east shore of the Lake averages about 28 inches. As the air climbs over the top of the Carson Range on the east side of the Lake, precipitation increases again; but there is less moisture available, and annual precipitation is only 38 inches at about the same elevation as that of the Sierra Nevada Crest.

The air has been wrung out twice by the time it reaches Carson City six miles east of the Carson Range Crest, and annual precipitation there is only about 11 inches. The air once again rises to cross the mountains east of town, but there is only marginally more precipitation — perhaps 15 inches annually.

Certain tree species are best adapted for certain microclimates, so the the tree species present, shown on the schematic diagram, also change. At the Sierra Nevada Crest, Red Fir and Lodgepole Pine dominate, and Western White Pine and Mountain Hemlock are also common. At Lake level, Jeffrey Pine and White Fir dominate on both shores. Atop the Carson Range, the same trees are present as on the Sierra Nevada Crest, because these trees are more sensitive to temperature changes than precipitation changes. The Carson Valley has no trees except river trees and planted trees. In the mountains east of Carson City, the only two species capable of thriving are Single-leaf Pinyon Pine and Utah Juniper.

Let us turn our attention back to other trees found at Lake level. These include Quaking Aspen, Black Cottonwood, willows, Incense Cedar, Ponderosa Pine, Lodgepole Pine and Sugar Pine. The first three types of trees are water-loving and are usually restricted to creek banks and beaches. Incense Cedar is found all arond the Lake but rarely dominates areas. Ponderosa Pine, the most widespread conifer of the western United States, thrives in warmer conditions than are found here, so it is near the top of its range (in fact, I have seen few trees more than 100 feet above Lake level). Lodgepole Pine, the second most widespread conifer of the West, is near the bottom of its range here. This leaves Sugar Pine, which dominates many stands within the Sierra Nevada at elevations from 3000 feet to 7000 feet. Why are less than one percent of Lake-level trees Sugar Pines? The answer, as they say, is history.

Early History of the Lake Tahoe Basin

Before the 1860s the few residents of this area left the forest relatively unscathed; but in 1859 gold was found in a massive strike at the Comstock Lode in Virginia City, a town only 30 miles east of the center of the Lake. With frenzied mining activity and the resultant influx of people, animals and trains, the Virginia City area was soon stripped of the small and sparse Single-leaf Pinyon and Utah Juniper trees. The mining industry needed wood for mining timbers, smelting operations, fuel, buildings and railroad ties; it turned its eyes west to the seemingly limitless Tahoe forest.

Lumber mills appeared, and trees disappeared at an astonishing rate until the mining boom ended in the 1880s, but by that time the once-beautiful Tahoe forest had been almost defoliated: the only places spared were those too difficult to log and the lakeside estates of wealthy individuals.

The trees you are seeing which all seem to be about the same size are about a hundred years old, the result of rapid forest regeneration after logging slowed down. This regeneration was probably too fast for healthy growth because tree stands are too thick to provide adequate light and moisture for all trees, and in the last few years insects have been killing these weakened trees at an alarming rate. Logging still continues, but now for a different reason: the dead trees are being salvaged, and dead trees along roads are cut down to decrease the possibility that they might fall on people and buildings.

If you were a logger a century or so ago, you would look for a tree which was large (providing a large volume of lumber), soft (so it could be cut down easily), and suitable for the uses mentioned above. Sugar Pine not only fits all these requirements; it also has a satiny finish which made beautiful interior wood. You can bet that the logger would cut a Sugar Pine first; the result is that there are no huge Sugar Pines except in preserved areas and those too remote for easy logging.

The second tree cut was Jeffrey Pine, followed by White Fir. Incense Cedar, with its twisted grain, was unsuitable for building lumber; its uses for fences and roof shingles required fewer trees, so many old trees remain.

There is no documentation of the original relative abundances of these species, so I'm going to guess at original figures (present figures are my estimates based on observation):

Species	Original Abundance	Present Abundance
Jeffrey Pine	60 %	64 %
Sugar Pine	30 %	1 %
White Fir	5 %	30 %
Incense Cedar	2 %	2 %
All Others	3 %	3 %
	100 %	100 %

This chart shows that White Fir abundance has increased tremendously. Why? My answer will come in a few minutes with the White Fir discussion. But first, Jeffrey Pine, whose features are sketched on the next page.

Jeffrey Pine

Find a Jeffrey Pine tree about 10 to 20 feet tall near you (the best place to look is at the edge of a driveway or road); I'll do the same. Note that there is a set of three to five horizontal branches at eye level starting from the same height on the trunk. Above and below eye level the same pattern is present. Above the top horizontal branch is a vertical branch, called the "leader."

Each spring Jeffrey Pine trees send out the leader and three to five horizontal shoots. All of these extend throughout the growing season. The next spring more horizontal shoots grow, starting at the top of the leader; this is convenient for us Tree Lovers, because we can tell how old the tree is by counting horizontal branches. (After the tree is about 25 years old, however, this method becomes impractical because it is hard to see the upper branches and because the lowest branches fall off)

In the second year of growth of a horizontal branch it often splits into two smaller branches; you may see some on your tree. Examine one of the lower horizontal branches from its tip to the trunk. You see an area of needles, then an area of no needles, then an area of needles, etc. This indicates the age of the branch — one year's growth is represented between the end of one set of needles and the end of the next set. Now find a branch and count how old it is. In the area of no needles the branch is thinner and darker.

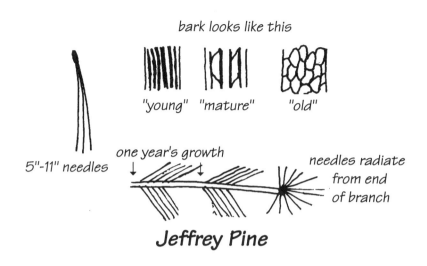

bark looks like this

"young"   "mature"   "old"

5"-11" needles   one year's growth   needles radiate from end of branch

Jeffrey Pine

Looking along the lower branches, you will eventually see no needles but instead diamond-shaped patterns. These are scars where needles were connected to the branch but fell off. Further toward the trunk there are no needle scars, because the bark has changed in appearance.

Now travel downward from the leader. Each year's growth has an area of needles on about the top half, and then no needles, etc., just like the horizontal branches. The needle scars disappear downward just as they did inward on the horizontal branches.

Jeffrey Pine needles stay on the tree for an average of only about seven years. This is because the function of the needles is to gather light, and needles toward the trunk or below the leader gather little light; so they are not necessary to the tree's operation and the tree sheds them.

Back to your young tree. Note that the trunk is a little wider beneath each horizontal branch. Healthy Jeffrey Pines grow wider and taller each year until they reach a certain height (about 150 feet in the Lake Tahoe Basin); however, width growth of both trunk and branches generally continues until the tree dies.

There is a fairly good correlation between diameter and height for the local Jeffrey Pines. The chart on the next page is based on my measurements of local trees; the line gives an average value. This chart is here because, for us Tree Lovers, it is easy to estimate tree diameter but difficult to estimate tree height. This chart should give you a ballpark figure for tree height.

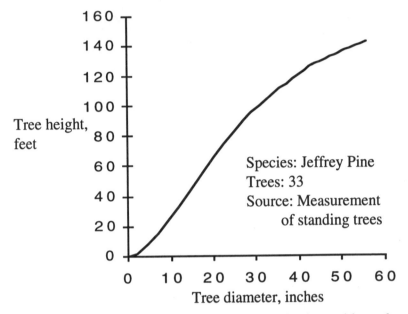

Species: Jeffrey Pine
Trees: 33
Source: Measurement
          of standing trees

Look up and down your tree. Are the horizontal branches evenly spaced? It is extremely unlikely. Usually the lowest branches of a young tree are a few inches apart; as the tree establishes itself later, its vertical growth increases (typically a foot to two feet per year).

Looking at my tree, I see one annual growth of two feet bracketed by growths of one foot. These trees don't increase height equally each year; they are sensitive to changing growing conditions. Was there a wet winter with plenty of moisture available during spring; was there a summer drought? Was it cold? Hot? Was the tree shaded by another tree? Was it a bad year for insects and the tree used up most of its energy just surviving? All these things and more could affect tree growth; so the height-versus-diameter chart represents an average of many trees rather than a specific tree.

Look at a horizontal branch for which you can count years. Note that horizontal growth is not as great as vertical growth; for example, the tree might have grown a foot taller but only a couple

of inches wider during that year. This makes sense if you
about it: if each year horizontal growth was as great as vertic
growth, the tree would be twice as wide as high! This would make
the tree unstable, with overly-long branches liable to break, and
the tree would compete for space with other trees in the forest. So
each species has an optimum width-to-height ratio for a given
situation. Some trees in this forest seem to be wider than others of
the same height; generally trees in open areas spread farther than
those in densely-populated areas. In your Adventures, you will
see this.

Bark

Look at your tree's bark. Near the top it is light gray and
smooth, with plentiful needles; at the base of the tree it is likely
dark brown to reddish brown, with vertical furrows about an inch
deep. If your tree has smooth bark, look at progressively larger
trees for change in bark appearance. When I did this I came up with
the following progression from the top to the bottom of the trunk:

Smooth light gray bark, needles
Smooth light gray bark, needle scars
Smooth light gray bark, no scars   (7 years from top)
Light gray bark with vertical cracks   (15 years)
Brownish dark gray bark, cracks deeper and wider (25
years)
Dark red brown bark, cracks deeper and wider (40 years)

When a Jeffrey Pine tree is about 100 to 150 years old, the
bark changes. The areas between the cracks become flat and
lighter-colored than before. In the next century or so, these lighter-
colored raised areas widen and the cracks start to disappear. The
bark pattern of an old tree (called"alligator bark") has polygonal
plates separated by cracks one to three inches both wide and deep.
Each tree has a unique bark pattern. If there is a nearby tree with
this bark appearance, it is an old Jeffrey Pine. Examine its bark;
within each polygonal plate are pieces of bark shaped like picture
puzzle pieces. Pry a piece off with your fingers; it won't hurt the
tree and it's fun to do. The red color on the underside of the piece
is characteristic of Jeffrey Pine.

So why does bark change in appearance and what does it do anyway? The answers will come when you find a Jeffrey Pine stump with bark on it. There are probably some near you, because many dead or dying local trees are cut down to avoid danger to people and property.

The diagram on the next page shows the parts of a tree trunk as seen on a stump. The wood of the trunk could be likened to a bundle of straws with other bundles above and below it. Each straw is one cell, called a "tracheid" in conifers. You might be able to see cross sections of indvidual tracheids on your stump, but generally tracheids are too small to be seen by the naked eye. In the outer part of the wood (called "sapwood"), tracheids act like little pipes, bringing from the tree's roots water containing elements such as sulfur and potassium necessary for tree growth.

The inner area of the wood, called "heartwood," conducts no fluids because the tree has filled the tracheids with resin, an epoxy-like substance. Heartwood provides strength to hold the tree up, much as your bones hold up your muscles.

The leaves are "food factories" — through many chemical reactions they make an amazing variety of materials for tree growth (for example: sugars, starches, fats, proteins, and en zymes), using as raw materials oxygen, water and carbon dioxide from air and fluids brought from the roots by the sapwood. These chemical reactions require that more energy be put in than comes out. The necessary energy is obtained via a marvelous substance called "chlorophyll," which changes sunlight energy into chemical energy to drive the reactions; the process of change is called "photosynthesis."

Stored in the leaves until ready for use, these growth materials eventually travel through the inner part of the bark (called "inner bark" or "phloem") to groups of cells which divide to provide tree growth. These are called "cambium" cells, and they divide throughout the growing season, requiring energy. This energy comes from chemical reactions changing the food materials back into water, carbon dioxide and oxygen.

There are two types of cambium cells. The ones between the wood and the bark are called "vascular cambium" cells; they divide into either two wood cells or a wood cell and a phloem cell. The phloem cell does not divide; the outer wood cell becomes the new cambium cell and the tree becomes just a little bit wider.

The other type of cambium cell is located within the bark; it divides into phloem and "outer bark" cells. The outer bark cells are lined with materials which make them waterproof, so nutrients cannot reach them. They are "dead," much as your hair or fingernails are.

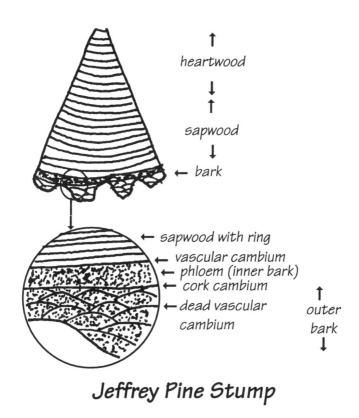

heartwood

sapwood

← bark

← *sapwood with ring*
← *vascular cambium*
← *phloem (inner bark)*
← *cork cambium*
← *dead vascular cambium*

outer bark

Jeffrey Pine Stump

What material can you think of that is soft, easily-shaped, lightweight and waterproof, such as you might find sealing a wine bottle? How about cork? "Cork" is another name for outer bark, and the cambium layer between inner and outer bark is called "cork cambium."

Although all trees have cork, the Cork Oak seems to be the principal tree for commercial cork. About every 10 years, Portuguese farmers strip the outer bark from each tree. It can't really be helping the tree, but the tree lives for another 10 years before the process is repeated.

As a Jeffrey Pine tree grows, the area around the cork cambium is stretched; it eventually breaks. The tree makes new cork cambium cells within the phloem; later the new cells are stretched and eventually break. So what works itself to the outside surface of the tree (the part that you see on a living tree) is a combination of cork cambium and phloem. Look at your stump. You will see scalloped pieces of bark. The porous-looking areas are the cork (which used to be phloem), and the thin darker areas are the area around the cork cambium.

The outer bark protects the inner parts of the tree from things which might harm the tree: dehydration (tree growth materials are dissolved in water; remove the water, the materials cannot move, and the tree doesn't grow); temperature extremes (if the tree is too hot, it cannot photosynthesize; if it is too cold, the water in the cells freezes, and the increase in volume during the conversion from water to ice ruptures the cells); falling branches; and pests (who would love to have a free lunch of tree nutrients).

Look at the wood rings on the stump. A wood ring has two parts: a lower, lighter-colored part and a raised, darker part. The lighter part, called "earlywood," is the result of cell division during spring when moisture is abundant, there is lots of sun and temperatures are reasonably mild (optimum conditions for photosynthesis); earlywood has large cells with thin walls. The raised part, called "latewood," is formed during summer, fall and winter when conditions are not optimum; cells are smaller with thicker cell walls. The greater proportion of solid materials makes latewood harder, so after sawing latewood rings stand out higher. Together the two different kinds of wood represent one year's growth, and form the wood grain which looks so beautiful in furniture or paneling. Some local trees (such as Quaking Aspen) have an indistinct grain and are more useful for chair legs and such where homogeneity is an asset.

For us Tree Adventurers, the best part about rings is that they enable us to tell how old the tree was when cut. Count 10 rings starting at the middle of the stump; this is how much the tree grew in the first 10 years. Now count the next 10 rings; I don't see your stump, but almost always the diameter increased more than in the first 10 years. Repeat this process for the rest of the stump.

The chart on the next page shows my measurements of Jeffrey Pine stumps around Lake Tahoe. This chart shows that diameter increases slowly for 10 to 20 years, accelerates until about 100 years, and slows again for the rest of the life of the tree.

But is tree growth really slowing down? What about height growth and tree volume?

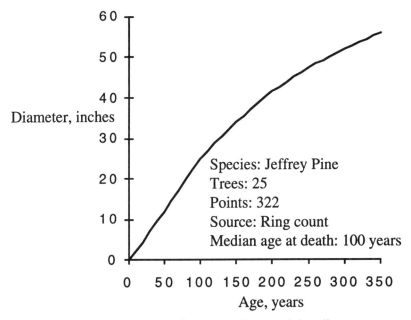

From the age-versus-diameter chart and the diameter-versus-height chart previously shown, age versus height can be plotted. The top chart on the next page shows tree height growth with age. This chart shows that, after the tree is about 10 years old, height grows at an almost constant rate until the tree is about 125 feet tall at 200 years old; height growth then slows.

If we know both height and diameter at a given age, we can calculate trunk volume using commonly accepted forestry industry equations for Ponderosa Pine, a tree very similar to Jeffrey Pine. The bottom chart on the next page, the result of those calculations, shows that volume growth per year is almost nil for the first 20 years, increases until about 100 years, then stays more or less constant through the life of the tree.

So what is all this volume growth for? The main job of a tree is to grow, and it needs energy to grow. This energy comes from photosynthesis, and this requires leaves. A tree 140 feet tall weighing several tons needs more energy than a tree 10 feet tall weighing perhaps 20 pounds. To make more leaves, a tree must

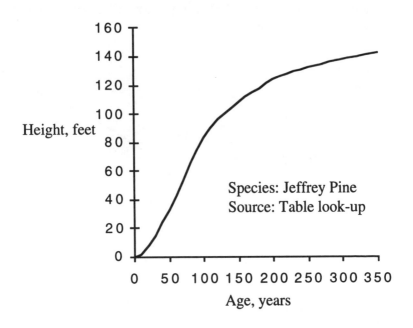

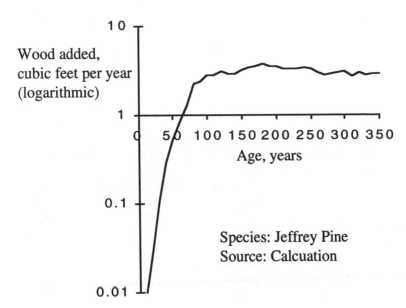

increase its number of branches (so now you know why there are split branches on your tree).

Trees over 250 years old are taller than younger smaller trees, so they must expend more energy in lifting water to the crown; also, because they are taller and because their branches are larger and heavier, wind, snow and lightning tend to break more branches. The tree must then repair or replace these branches. Also, insects and fungi are attacking the wounds, so the tree must expend a lot of energy to ward off these attacks.

Appendix F includes a listing of a 300-year-old Jeffrey Pine's energy budget.

Incidentally, notice from the graph that, for the tree stumps I measured, the median age of death (life expectancy) is 100 years. This age for "second-growth forest" is very close to my results from the Ponderosa Pines of Yosemite Valley, another "second-growth forest."

A disclaimer here: my measurements are not the result of a rigorously scientific study — you could do the same as I; they are the result of my curiosity about how local trees grow. Actually, I have never seen such a study in the literature, so I'll stay with my results (which were a lot of fun for me to obtain).

Besides height, volume and age, trees have other amazing dimensions. Appendix F gives the dimensions of a typical large Jeffrey Pine tree.

Cones

Look on the ground for cones. The cones around you probably have different apprearances. Some are small, heavy and tight; others have been savagely attacked; still others are large and symmetrical and would look good on your mantel. These three appearances are indicative of what has happened to the cone.

For some reason or other, the small tight cones have not matured. It may be because wind knocked them off the tree, insects attacked them or squirrels nibbled them. These cones normally fall in spring.

Cones destroyed on the ground were probably cut off the tree by squirrels. Squirrels have to chew the cone scales off to get to the nutritious seeds hidden within, and in the process destroy the cones. Timing is important: in September, many Jeffrey Pine cones open and the seeds twirl down to the ground. If the squirrel is eating or storing seeds then, no cones need be cut. But both earlier and later in the year, the squirrel must remove cone scales to eat. (Seeds are only about one percent of cone weight and are a lot easier for the squirrel to store; also, durnig most of the winter snow covers cones)

The symmetrical unscathed cones survived to full size and the tree severed its connection with them, having no need for them after their seeds were shed.

Let's put this cone destruction into perspective. An old-age Jeffrey Pine may have made a million seeds in its lifetime, all to replace itself with one more tree. If all the seeds in one cone germinated, there would be a tiny forest around the mother tree; if they all grew to, say, 50 feet tall, the forest would be impenetrable and the tree trunks would be touching.

All the things that destroy cones and prevent seeds from sprouting are actually beneficial, and keep the forest from being overwhelmed with trees. This is why I don't get very concerned when I hear about forests being decimated by bark beetle kills or forest fires; these trees have such regenerative power they will come back in the long run, if not in our lifetimes. (About 100 years ago Tahoe was denuded of trees; look at today's beautiful forest. I rest my case.)

White Fir

Now that you've become intimate with Jeffrey Pine, look for a White Fir tree. There is probably one within sight. To help you find one I have included a sketch below.

Although it is a less popular Christmas tree in the West than its close relative Red Fir, about 2 percent of U. S. Christmas trees are Whte Fir. Why? The answer can be found out by describing what people want in a Christmas tree. For a six-foot tree, they want about eight to ten horizontal branches, with a lot of splits along the branch so they can hang more ornaments and provide a framework for lights strung around the tree; fairly stiff branches capable of holding ornaments; short needles which don't hide ornaments; needles which don't fall off in the first two days; and a nice smell. White Fir has no smell, but meets the rest of the qualifications. A Jeffrey Pine would make a poor tree: it grows vertically too fast, has few splits in the horizontal branches, the branches are not stiff

enough; and the needles are so long that they would hide ornaments.

The top third of the branches of a medium or large White Fir
tree point upward, the middle third are horizontal, and the bottom
third droop downward. This is true not only for White Fir but also
for most conifers in the Sierra Nevada forest. I haven't seen an
explanation for this; my guess is that as branches get older, they
get bigger, and gravity takes its toll.

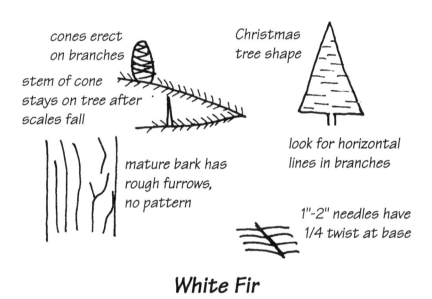

*cones erect
on branches*

*stem of cone
stays on tree after
scales fall*

*Christmas
tree shape*

*mature bark has
rough furrows,
no pattern*

*look for horizontal
lines in branches*

*1"-2" needles have
1/4 twist at base*

White Fir

White Fir cones differ from Jeffrey Pine cones in three
respects, as shown in the table below.

	White Fir	Jeffrey Pine
Cone orientation	vertical	horizontal or drooping
Cones on ground	rare (usually disin-tegrate on tree)	plentiful
Cones on tree	only top 1/3 or 1/4	entire tree

My measurements of age-versus-diameter and height-versus-diameter show that these trees grow at about the same rate as Jeffrey Pines.

Finally, the answer to the question I posed about why White Fir has become more abundant in the Lake Tahoe Basin in the last century: When the Tahoe forests were logged only a few Jeffrey Pine and White Fir trees deemed too deformed or diseased to log were left to seed; and except for stumps and "slash" — sawdust, broken branches and needles — the ground was open. In the next year or two, wildflower, pine and fir seeds germinated. But Jeffrey Pine germinates best on bare soil, and the former forest floor was littered with debris. White Fir is less picky about soil conditions, so it germinated better. The shade of opportunistically encroaching wildflowers and shrubs was worse for Jeffrey Pine than for White Fir, because White Fir is more tolerant of shade. Still, the original ratio of Jeffrey Pine to White Fir was pretty high, so despite adverse growing conditions Jeffrey Pine is more abundant today.

In this Adventure we barely moved, but found out a lot about the life of trees. And now that you know some things about a typical tree, you will be able to enjoy the other Adventures more.

ADVENTURE 2

From South Lake Tahoe to Tahoe City

This Adventure starts at the South Lake Tahoe "Y" (see the map in the Foreword for orientation). A left turn on U. S. 50 leads to Placerville and Sacramento; our route, a right turn on California 89, leads to Tahoe City. Mileages will give you an approximate idea of when the various sights will occur. After a mile or so, you leave "Civilization" and enter the forest.

Appendix A gives the demographics for commmunities along this Adventure.

As in the other Adventures, there are two sets of numbers at the left side of the page. The number outside the parentheses is mileage from the start of the Adventure; the number inside the parentheses is the distance between notations.

3.1 (3.1) The road to the right leads to the Tallac Historic Site, and 0.1 mile ahead another road turns to the right to the U. S. Forest Service Visitor Center. These places are so interesting in terms of trees and other things that Side Trip A has been set up for this area; it is in Appendix H.

The road to the left goes to Fallen Leaf Lake, at three miles by one mile the largest lake near Lake Tahoe. A natural dam formed by glacial action (a terminal moraine) impounded the water in this lake. There is a glacial moraine a couple of miles ahead on this Adventure.

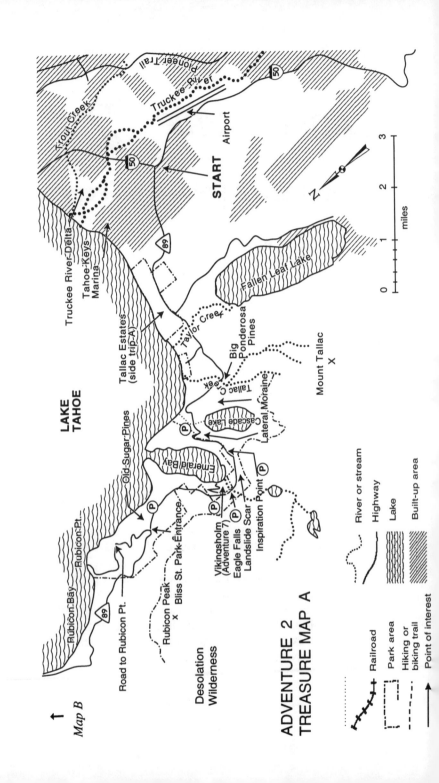

ADVENTURE 2
TREASURE MAP A

Map B

LAKE
TAHOE

START
Airport

Truckee River
Pioneer Trail

Trout Creek

50

50

89

Truckee River Delta

Tahoe Keys Marina

Tallac Estates (side trip-A)

Old Sugar Pines

Taylor Creek

Big Ponderosa Pines

Fallen Leaf Lake

Tallac Creek

Mount Tallac X

Cascade Lake

Lateral Moraine

Emerald Bay

Inspiration Point

Vikingsholm (Adventure 7)

Eagle Falls

Landslide Scar

Bliss St. Park Entrance

Rubicon Peak X

Road to Rubicon Pt.

Rubicon Bay

Rubicon Pt.

89

Desolation Wilderness

N

0   1   2   3
miles

River or stream

Highway

Lake

Built-up area

Railroad

Park area

Hiking or biking trail

Point of interest

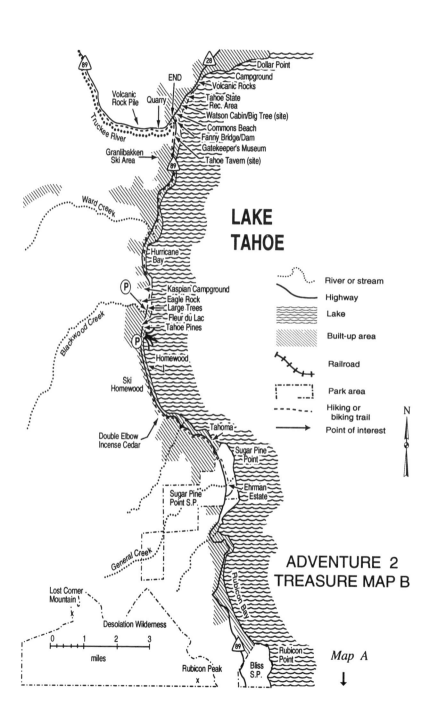

89

28 Dollar Point

Volcanic Rock Pile

Quarry

END

Campground
Volcanic Rocks
Tahoe State
Rec. Area
Watson Cabin/Big Tree (site)
Commons Beach
Fanny Bridge/Dam
Gatekeeper's Museum
Tahoe Tavern (site)

Truckee River

Granlibakken
Ski Area

89

Ward Creek

LAKE
TAHOE

Hurricane
Bay

P

Kaspian Campground
Eagle Rock
Large Trees
Fleur du Lac
Tahoe Pines

Blackwood Creek

P

Homewood

Ski
Homewood

Double Elbow
Incense Cedar

Tahoma

Sugar Pine
Point

Ehrman
Estate

Sugar Pine
Point S.P.

General Creek

Rubicon Bay

Lost Corner
Mountain

x

Desolation Wilderness

0   1   2   3

miles

Rubicon Peak

x

89

Bliss
S.P.

Rubicon
Point

······· River or stream

——— Highway

≈≈≈ Lake

//// Built-up area

+—+— Railroad

·—·—· Park area

- - - Hiking or
biking trail

——➤ Point of interest

N

ADVENTURE 2
TREASURE MAP B

Map A

↓

4.5 (1.4)   On the left edge of the highway is a huge old **Ponderosa Pine**. This fourth largest Ponderosa Pine around the Lake is 6.2 feet in diameter and 145 feet tall (the third largest is about 100 feet away on the other side of the highway). Ponderosa Pines are first cousins of Jeffrey Pine, and this tree exhibits the bark characteristic of "old" trees. Jeffrey and Ponderosa Pines are difficult to distinguish from a distance, since they appear so similar; but the table below shows some of the differences between them.

Feature	Ponderosa Pine	Jeffrey Pine
Bark odor	No odor	Smells like vanilla
Cone size	Generally smaller (4"-6")	Generally larger (6"-8")

The highway descends to the floodplain for Tallac Creek, one of 64 creeks emptying into Lake Tahoe (see Adventure 5 for a discussion of floodplains). The types of trees here, present in nearly all the drainages into the Lake are Black Cottonwood, willows and Quaking Aspen. A few miles ahead we will look at these trees in more detail.

6.4 (1.9)   As you head uphill past this 10-mile-per-hour "hairpin curve," think about the difficulty of not only building roads here (this was the last part of the highway built around Lake Tahoe) but also keeping them maintained (this section of the highway often is closed in winter). At the top of this hill is another hairpin curve with a turnout on the right. Pull off onto the dirt turnout and look back behind you at Cascade Lake. It's called that because of the beautiful cascade at the upper end of the lake which brightens up the early summer vista.

About 0.7 milesfarther, after two more hairpin turns, the highway flattens and the hill slopes precipitously to Cascade Lake on the left side and Emerald Bay on the right side. The view is exciting from atop this flat-topped hill deposited by glaciers, but the hill is only about 30 feet wide. Since there is no parking area at roadside, it is an awful place to stop; a better one is the Inspiration Point Parking Area.

7.7 (1.3) Pull into the Inspiration Point Parking Area on the right. This area of the West Shore of Lake Tahoe has mountains reaching 9000 feet, or about 2500 feet above you (you are about 500 feet above the Lake).

Emerald Bay, Cascade Lake and the hill you just drove on were created by glacial action. Here's how: In the Ice Age, the temperature was colder with more snow than today; in fact, more snow fell on these mountains than melted. Snow is funny stuff. When it gets thicker than about 150 feet thick (such as in the valleys which now contain Cascade Lake and Emerald Bay), snow turned to ice flows downhill in response to gravity, much as an extremely slow-moving river. At the edge of the ice, frost action knocks rocks from the mountainside onto the ice, and the ice river acts as a giant conveyor belt for these rocks. Also, the combination of slow-moving ice and imbedded rocks acts like a giant sheet of sandpaper to remove even more rocks from the mountainsides, from boulder-size to microscopic. Where two glaciers meet (such as in the area between Cascade Lake and Emerald Bay), the two conveyer belts meet and concentrate the rock in a line (in this case, heading northeast).

The sandpaper action also occurs at the bottom of the river of glacial ice. Where the rocks are weaker, it scours more deeply. Emerald Bay and Cascade Lake are the result of this scouring. In all mountain glaciers, ice and rocks head downslope to a place where more snow melts than falls, and the ice melts. This is the front of the glacier. Here the conveyor belt stops, dumping a huge pile of rock. Where this rockpile goes across the entire valley, a natural lake may form because the smaller rocks plug up holes in the dam and water is trapped behind it; this is what happened at Fallen Leaf Lake and Squaw Valley and Washoe and Donner Lakes of Adventure 5.

In places where the underlying rock is very strong, the glacier rides over the rock and creates what geologists term a "roche moutonee." Fannette Island, in the middle of Emerald Bay, is an example of a roche moutonee. The downhill slope of the roche moutonee is typically greater than the uphill slope.

All glaciers eventually have less snowfall than snowmelt; in the Cascade Lake-Emerald Bay area, the ice melted from around the northeast-trending conveyor belt rock fragments, and dumped them into place. The result was the long, flat-topped straight ridge of glacial material called a "lateral moraine" such as that on which you just drove.

Across the highway is the trailhead for Bayview Trail, which after a few hundred yards has nice views of Cascade Lake.

A few hundred yards farther along the highway is a bare area with only a few small trees, the scar from two major landslides in the 1950s. There is a small turnout on the right just past the scar, but it has room for only two or three cars. If you can't park there, proceed to the small parking lot on the left at the bottom of the hill (the trailhead for Eagle Falls and Eagle Lakes Trail). If you can't park there, proceed up the hill to the Vikingsholm parking lot.

In this area, zones of weakness in the rocks (called "joints") have an angle very close to that of the mountainside, and an unstable situation exists; but Man has worsened it. In order to construct Highway 89 through the Emerald Bay area in 1913, road builders cut into the mountain, oversteepening Nature's already unstable slope. All that was needed for rock failure was a very snowy winter. In the winter of 1953 a massive landslide occurred, starting about 300 feet above the highway and going down almost to Lake level. In the winter of 1955-56 the mountainside failed in the same place, this time resulting in a larger landslide starting 200 feet higher. Two hundred thousand cubic yards of mountain — enough to fill a city block to a depth of 19 feet — slid downhill, closing the highway through the next summer. (These landslides were puny in comparison with the ones which have occurred on Slide Mountain — which we pass on Adventure 5 — over geologic time; about 600 times as much material — enough to cover one square mile 120 feet deep — has slid off Slide Mountain)

There are only small trees in the landslide area, as compared with much larger trees on each side of the area. The slide removed all the soil and all the trees, and the small trees which germinated later are having a difficult time trying to grow in poor soil conditions.

At the bottom of the landslide area there is a dense stand of water-loving willow, Mountain Alder and Quaking Aspen trees. Water probably percolates underground through the slide material to these trees.

Two other recent landslide or avalanche areas are visible from here. Past the Vikingsholm parking lot area about a quarter mile ahead on the highway is another area with only shrubs and small trees surrounded by larger trees. This is the result of a smaller landslide in 1980; if you go on Adventure 7, you will actually cross this area. To its right is another area of small trees, caused by an avalanche in 1982. There are other areas with shrubs and small trees on the mountain above Vikingsholm; obviously this is an area with unstable ground.

This is one of the most-photographed areas of the Lake (look for it on postcards while you're at lunch).

8.6 (0.9) On the left side of the highway is a parking lot for hikes to Eagle Falls and Eagle Lake. Eagle Falls, the only waterfall you can see from the Lake, looks more impressive from its base (easily reached by hiking a foot trail from Vikingsholm); however, the top of the waterfall is only a few yards away across the highway if you can find a parking place.

Eagle Lake is a 1.0 mile hike from the trailhead at this parking lot. The lake is at the edge of one of the the least-wild Wilderness Areas in the country (the Desolation Wilderness), and Eagle Falls Trail is one of the more popular entries to the Desolation Wilderness. Each summer day, thousands of hikers and backpackers enter the Wilderness.

About 0.2 miles ahead on the right is the parking lot for Vikingsholm, a replica of a Norse fortress of circa 1300 A.D. This is the starting point for Adventure 7, which features water-loving trees and shrubs and three of the biggest individual trees in the Lake Tahoe Basin. The concrete and rock walls on the left side of the highway for the next half mile were built to stabilize the hillside and to keep rocks from falling onto the highway.

During winter, this stretch of highway is frequently closed after snowstorms because of the threat of avalanches. As you can see from looking at the mountainside, there is no place to go when the avalanche is coming, and the avalanche will be upon you in a matter of seconds.

10.2 (1.6) This is the start of a two-mile-long stretch of old-growth Sugar Pine trees. The best of several turnouts along the highway is on the right side at 10.2 miles (look for a hill between the highway and the Lake). From there you can walk a few feet to an area dominated by old Sugar Pines.

Sugar Pine is easily recognizable most of the year by the foot-long cones hanging straight down from the ends of the longest branches of any pine. Branches with several of the heavy cones droop gracefully in an arc which distinguishes Sugar Pine from all other Tahoe trees.

Besides the cones, several features of Sugar Pine differ from those of Jeffrey Pine. Sugar Pine has five needles in a bundle, rather than three, and the needles are much shorter; needles radiate from spots all along the branches rather than from the ends of branches; the branches are very long, extending in all directions (I call this "arms akimbo"); and the branches don't split into smaller branches as much as Jeffrey Pine's. The result of these last three characteristics is that the foliage of Sugar Pine seems sparser than that of Jeffrey Pine.

When Sugar Pine bark is injured, the tree exudes a sap which gives the tree its name. The syrup made from this sap, in John Muir's mind, rivalled maple syrup for taste.

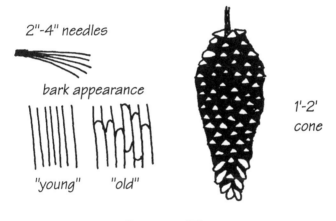

2"-4" needles

bark appearance

"young"   "old"

1'-2' cone

Sugar Pine

The Sugar Pines around here range from young trees with branches sweeping optimistically upward to old grizzled veterans of many a harsh winter, dry summer and insect attack. The oldsters don't have a beautiful symmetrical shape, but they are I think they are magnificent. What do you think?

This area is one of the few at Lake Tahoe with an old-growth forest ruled by the noble Sugar Pine. The abundance of old Sugar Pine trees here is due partly to a topography too rugged for logging the giant trees, but also due to its presence on the estate of Duane Bliss, a Tahoe legend who capitalized on the Comstock Lode gold and silver boom in the last century as a mining, railroading and lumber magnate.

In 1929 the Bliss Family donated 744 acres in this area to the state park system, and it is now Bliss State Park; the park entrance is 0.5 miles ahead. One park road leads to Rubicon Point, a rocky headland above the Lake. One quarter mile offshore from the point, the water is 1440 feet deep — an incredible underwater slope of almost 45 degrees! This slope may be the scarp of one of the 45-degree faults which created Lake Tahoe. Lake Tahoe is a "graben," a block dropped when the blocks on each side spread — in fact, the bottom of the Lake is 150 feet lower than Carson City The block was higher on the south side, and when the volcanic flows around Tahoe City dammed the entire north side of the graben, Lake Tahoe was born.

12.3 (2.1) The presence of houses marks the end of Bliss State Park. This is one of the most prestigious (equals expensive) areas around the Lake. It is probably desirable for two reasons: Rubicon Bay to your right has blue-green water reminiscent of the Caribbean; and this area is remote from "civilization" (15 miles from Tahoe City and 12 miles from the South Lake Tahoe "Y").

17.4 (5.1) The road to the right is the entrance to Sugar Pine Point State Park, another formerly privately-held estate acquired in 1975. The features of this place making it worthy of a visit are the Ehrman Mansion (a turn-of-the-century "summer house"), "the highest lighthouse in the nation", a log cabin built of Incense Cedar in 1872, and a nature trail along the beach with many fine old Incense Cedars and Sugar Pines. Despite its name, the park contains relatively few huge Sugar Pines, because a logging operation active here from 1865 to 1877 removed big trees from everywhere except the higher ridges. About a half mile farther along the highway is a trail leading from a campground into the Desolation Wilderness.

18.5 (1.1) At the end of the park the town of Tahoma marks the beginning of a residential area which is almost continuous all the way to Incline Village. Note that the houses were built within the forest, disturbing as few trees as possible.

20.4 (1.9) Just past Meadow Road on the left is a cinnamon-barked tree with a double elbow. Old **Incense Cedars** commonly have elbows, but this is the only one I have ever seen with a double elbow; apparently the main trunk was killed by lightning, and the elbows carry on the growth of the tree. This tree marks the beginning of a stretch of old Incense Cedars, our next featured tree. The best place to see this tree (and some other things) is on the other end of Homewood, 1.4 miles ahead.

About 0.6 miles ahead on the left is Ski Homewood, one of only three Lakeside skiing areas out of the 24 skiing areas in the area of these Adventures. The bottom of the skiing runs are only about 200 feet from the Lake, in one of the snowiest areas of the Lakeshore; but since this is the lowest-elevation skiing area in the Truckee River Basin, it sometimes rains here when it snows in higher elevation skiing areas.

21.8 (1.4) As you see the beach ahead, look for Cherry Street and park on it, because this is an area of plentiful old Incense Cedar trees.

Because of similar bark colors, many people mistake Incense Cedar for Coast Redwood, Giant Sequoia or Sierra Juniper. But Coast Redwood is only native to the fog-bound California and Oregon coasts; and though Giant Sequoia is native to the Sierra Nevada, Lake Tahoe does not have any of the 75 remaining native groves of this species. The climate is good for Giant Sequoia here, but every Giant Sequoia tree in the Lake Tahoe Basin has been planted here. As a result, there are no old ones. The largest of the three Giant Sequoias in the arboretum at the Tallac Estate (Side Trip A) is 110 feet high, but it was planted in the twentieth century and is still a "baby." The only Sierra

Junipers along the route circling the Lake are near Vikingsholm (Adventure 7).

Look at one of the old trees. Incense Cedar foliage is drooping, many-branched, fan-shaped and light green. It does not send out horizontal branches and a leader each year like pines and firs, so it is difficult to tell how old a particular tree is. The few cones you might see under your tree don't look like pine cones; they are shaped like inch-long fleur-de-lis.

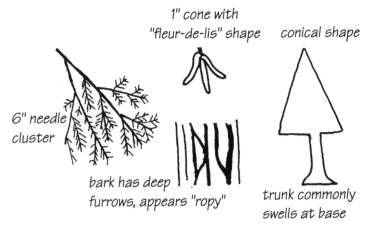

1" cone with "fleur-de-lis" shape

conical shape

6" needle cluster

bark has deep furrows, appears "ropy"

trunk commonly swells at base

Incense Cedar

These trees bear little resemblance to pines and firs because they are part of a different family, the Cypress Family, whose members include Cedars, Junipers and Cypresses.

Incense Cedar is not very useful for lumber, because its grain is so twisted that it does not saw well. It is useful for roof shingles and fence posts because of its durability, and for pier pilings because it does not rot readily (even in standing water). But one of its uses today might astound you. Do you have a Ticonderoga Number 2 pencil in your pocket? All of these are now made of Incense Cedar. Look at this tree and estimate how many pencils could be made from it, at 1/4 inch in diameter and eight inches long.

So are Incense Cedar trees used for building the many Tahoe cedar houses? No, those houses are built of Western Redcedar, which comes from Washington and Oregon.

The Incense Cedar trees in this area show how their bark changes with age. Young trees (which you can recognize by their foliage) have gray, fibrous bark which peels off in strips; older trees have hard, brown, furrowed bark; and the oldest trees have very hard cinnamon-colored bark. Old trees may have two interesting bark features. The first feature is black fire scars; the six-inch-thick bark of old Incense Cedars insulates the tree from forest fires (very few of which have occurred in the Lake Tahoe Basin since the coming of the white man 150 years ago). The bark contains tannin, a substance used to tan hides which is not only flame-retardant but is also unpalatable to insects. The second feature is small holes in the bark, because insects eventually get into the bark on their way to the nutritious inner bark and sapwood; birds such as woodpeckers peck into the bark to eat the nutritious insects. Some trees have many small holes in the bark, evidence of the bird's search for food.

So how old are these trees? The bark will give some clues as to the age, which may be more than 600 years. The diameter may also help. But the best way is to count rings on a stump. The oldest one I have seen in the Lake Tahoe Basin is 650 years old (see Adventures 3 and 9).

Since you're parked, this is a good place for a Lake vista. Starting from the right, the low land projection on the right is the largest one on the West Shore, Sugar Pine Point. To its left the highest peak is Freel Peak, at 10778 feet the highest peak in the area of these Tree Adventures. The low point in the mountains is Daggett Pass, about 3400 feet lower. Directly above Cave Rock (the tan-colored round-topped rock on the East Shore) is Genoa Peak. Just to the right of the next low point (Spooner Summit) is Duane Bliss Peak; the two peaks left of Spooner Summit are Snow Valley and Marlette Peaks, respectively. Behind Diamond Peak Ski Area is Slide Mountain. Across the next low point, Mount Rose Summit, is Mount Rose, the second tallest mountain in the area of these Adventures. At Lake level just to its right is Stateline Point with the Cal-Neva Lodge plainly visible. The last peak visible before the middleground mountainside cuts off ourt view is Martis Peak. Below this peak is Dollar Point.

A few hundred yards away on the Lakeshore are some strange-looking buildings. These are part of an estate built in 29 days in 1939 by 300 workmen in the employ of Henry J. Kaiser, the industrialist of Kaiser Aluminum and Jeep fame. Fleur du Lac (French for "flower of the lake") was built to house executives of Kaiser Aluminum during business meetings; in the last few years it has been sold and turned into eight condominiums. You could buy one of those strange-looking buildings; the going rate is $1.8 million.

As you drive north, look at the forbidding-looking fence on the right. This is part of the wall of Fleur du Lac.

About 0.3 miles ahead the highway crosses Blackwood Creek. Park in the turnout on the left side of the highway. This is the best place to examine three new trees, willow, Quaking Aspen and Black Cottonwood.

The Sierra Nevada has at least 11 native species of willows, and several are found along streams such as this one. As a group, they have a clump of thin trunks coming from the ground, with dense branches.The sketch on a following page shows some of the features of willows.

Quaking Aspen (see the sketch on a following page) is the tall, thin, white to greenish-light-yellow tree along Blackwood Creek's banks; it is probably the most widespread tree in North America. Native to the entire southern half of Canada and eastern United States, it also occurs in all mountain ranges from the Rockies westward. Its name comes from the fact that the leaves flutter ("quake") in even the slightest breeze.

Quaking Aspen grows in all soil types and at all elevations from sea level to tree line. In the Lake Tahoe Basin, this water-loving tree is usually found on moist hillsides and along rivers and creeks.

Although individual trees here only live about 100 years. Quaking Aspen is interesting in its ability to regenerate. After a tree-killing event such as a forest fire or logging, the still-live roots send up "root suckers," new trees coming from the ground around the "dead" tree. Since these new trees are actually part of the old tree, they have the same DNA and are actually clones of the old tree! The clones may cover 1/4 acre, and all sprout spring growth, flower and turn color at the same time. If you are here in late September or October, you can confirm this and have a wonderful visual show of flaming yellows and oranges at the same time.

The other tree common along all the creeks and rivers of the Truckee River Basin is **Black Cottonwood**, actually a member of the same genus as Quaking Aspen. Black Cottonwood (see the sketch on the next page) has gray bark; trunks of mature trees are round with straight vertical furrows about an inch wide and deep.

Cottonwood is so named because around June the tree sheds seeds surrounded by fluffy cotton-like fibers; the fluffy seeds are carried far away from the tree by wind. There is so much fluff that the tree would probably be a nuisance if it was planted in your yard.

Before you get back into your vehicle, look back past Blackwood Creek at the Jeffrey Pine in a residential yard. This tree, at 200 feet tall, is possibly the tallest tree you will see in these Tree Adventures (Adventure 9 gives its size).

3"-6" leaves are usually long and thin

usually less than 20' tall

old trees have many shoots sprouting from ground or trunk

Willows

weak stem allows leaf to twirl in wind

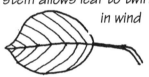

few branches below tops of young trees

straight white or greenish white trunk with horizontal lines

Quaking Aspen

mature bark is gray with straight black furrows

upper leaves

4"-6" leaves

lower leaves

Black Cottonwood

The hill ahead on the left side of the highway is Eagle Rock, the remnant of an ancient volcano. Volcanic material comes out of a hole called the "neck"; when a volcano finally becomes inactive, usually some material cools and solidifies in this hole. If this material is more resistant to erosion (as in this case), it is all that remains of the volcano.

The large boulder on the right side of the highway about 0.1 mile ahead is a piece of that volcanic neck. There are two other large volcanic necks along highways in the Lake Tahoe Basin: Cave Rock (site of the tunnel on U. S. 50; see Adventure 4), and Shakespeare Rock (near U.S. 50 south of its intersection with Nevada 28).

23.4 (1.0) The road on the left leads to Kaspian Campground, which can accommodate people in wheelchairs. Of the 25 Lake Tahoe Basin campgrounds, both publicly- and privately-owned, only Kaspian and one other (Nevada Beach on othe East Shore) have facilities for wheelchairs.

This campsite also appeals to bicyclists. Not only are there hundreds of miles of mountain biking trails around the Lake, but also there is a paved bike trail on the left side of the highway for families and people who want their exercise in smaller doses. This trail extends from the southern end of Sugar Pine Point State Park to Tahoe City (about eleven miles), where it splits just before the end of this Adventure; one branch follows California 28 for about two miles, and the other follows California 89 for five miles to Squaw Creek.

For those both brave enough to contend with vehicle traffic and fit enough for a longer road bike ride, there is always the 72-mile route circling the Lake. There are actually around-the-Lake races.

The bay on the right is locally known as "Hurricane Bay." I didn't know why until a November day when strong winds blew from the east side of the Lake. Wind blowing across a long distance of water (called "fetch") tends to make larger waves. If the water bottom topography is just right, the water tends to be concentrated from a large area into a small area and large waves result. On that November day, there were waves of four to six feet pounding on the shore. If there is a strong easterly wind, this is definitely the best place to be on the Lake shore.

Beaches with large storm wave heights tend to contain large, rounded rocks, because the turbulent water washes away all the sand and silt. For that reason, this is the one of the few beaches on the Lake with essentially no sand.

26.8 (3.4) On the right is a sign for Tahoe Tavern Shores, a gated condominium community along the Lake shore. This is the site of the Tahoe Tavern, a 283-room resort built by Duane Bliss. From 1901 until it was torn down in 1964, the Tahoe Tavern was a popular resort for Lake Tahoe vacationers. Travelers coming from the San Francisco Bay Area rode a standard-gauge train to Truckee and a narrow-gauge train from Truckee to Tahoe City; a spur delivered passengers to the resort's door. The train stopped on a pier about a quarter mile long; this pier is still the longest one on the Lake. The railroad was discontinued in 1943 because of improved road transportation and because rails were needed elsewhere for wartime activities; the bike trail from Tahoe City to Squaw Creek (see Adventure 5) travels along the old roadbed.

By the 1920s, winter travel to Tahoe was becoming more popular, and so were winter sports. Starting in 1929, Tahoe Tavern guests skied at Granlibakken, the first major ski resort in what is now one of the major ski destinations of the world (24 major downhill ski areas in or next to the Truckee River Basin, about the same as in the entire state of Colorado — see sidebar for details on ski areas). Granlibakken still operates; Granlibakken Road to the left leads to it in one mile.

****

Skiing

The first person to ski much at Lake Tahoe was the legendary skiing mailman, "Snowshoe" Thompson, a Norwegian native who got a job carrying mail to Lake Tahoe Basin residents in the late 1850s. For winter travel he fashioned a pair of skis out of boards and took off across the Sierra from the Sacramento Valley. People are still wondering how he survived over 20 years of winter trips across the Sierra Nevada.

With tourist trade increasing in the early 1900s, the winter sports skiing, sledding and tobogganing became popular. One of the best ways to get to Lake Tahoe was the railroad from Truckee to Tahoe City, and once there Tahoe Tavern guests there would ski in the area west of the Tavern. By 1929 there was enough business so that the first major ski resort — Granlibakken — could open nearby. The 1932 Olympic Ski Jump Trials were held there.

By the mid-1950s, several resorts had opened, including Heavenly Valley and Soda Springs. But things changed radically when Alex Cushing convinced U.S. officials to have them host the 1960 Winter Olympics at his small hill (with only one chair!) at Squaw Valley. These games, the first winter games televised, captivated the American public, and Tahoe was established as a major skiing destination.

Today, the Truckee River Basin and Donner Pass area form the largest concentration of ski resorts in the nation. Two of the nation's four largest resorts (Squaw Valley and Heavenly Valley) have a capacity of hundreds of thousands of skiers.

— Additional information in "A History of Squaw Valley" by Jane Fiedler

****

27.4 (0.6)   Fanny Bridge is probably named for the parts of the anatomy visible (from California 89) when people lean over the bridge to catch a glimpse of the numerous rainbow trout and other fish living here during the summer. The dam a few feet upstream from it has been the center of one of the most interesting controversies in the area (see sidebar for more detail).

The parking lot on the right just before the bridge is a good place from which to check out the bridge, the Gatekeeper's Museum, and the town of Tahoe City.

This Adventure ends at the traffic light just past the bridge. A left turn leads toward Truckee (the opposite direction is detailed in Adventure 5); a right turn leads toward Incline Village (detailed in Adventure 3).

****

Water Use and The Dam at Tahoe City

The most precious resource of the American West is not silver, gold or oil; it is WATER. Through the dam at Tahoe City each year passes an average of 57 billion gallons of this resource.

Since the 1860s, a number of parties have been trying to obtain that water. In 1870 a Mr. von Schmidt bought the land here and constructed a small wooden dam. His idea was to build an aqueduct from Lake Tahoe to San Francisco. Nevada farmers also wanted the water for irrigating crops in their desert land. And mill owners in Truckee needed water for floating logs to mills in Truckee (fort which the dam owners exacted a toll). By 1915, when the government acquired title to the dam, the property had passed through the hands of three more owners.

The present dam was constructed in 1913, and during severe water shortages in 1912, 1924 and 1930 there were attempts by Nevada farmers to illegally cut a channel alongside the dam and send water down the Truckee River. These attempts were met with considerable hostility and lawsuits by Lake residents, who did not think highly of their docks being left high and dry and their property values diminished by Nevada farmers.

In 1935 a compromise was worked out whereby Boca Reservoir was built near Truckee to supply water to farmers in drought times, the Bureau of Reclamation "owned" Lake Tahoe water from the natural rim of 6223 feet to 6229 feet (the not inconsiderable amount of about 250 billion gallons).

Next to the dam was the cabin of the gatekeeper, a person who physically opened and shut the gates when directed to do so. This cabin burned down in 1968, and the museum here today was built in 1981.

— Additional information in "Tahoe: An Environmental History

****

ADVENTURE 3

Tahoe City to Incline Village

This Adventure starts at the "Y" in Tahoe City (the intersection of California 89 and California 28), continues past the California-Nevada state line where the route number changes to Nevada 28, and ends at the intersection of Nevada 431 (Mount Rose Highway) and Nevada 28 (see the map in the Foreword for orientation). This stretch of the Lakeshore road is 14.2 miles long, of which 3.5 miles is one settlement or another.

Appendix A gives the demographics for communities along this Adventure.

As in the other Adventures, there are two sets of numbers at the left side of the page. The number outside the parentheses is mileage from the start of the Adventure; the number inside the parentheses is the distance between notations.

0.0 (0.0) Turn right (east) at the "Y". You are now in Tahoe City, and are probably in the middle of a traffic jam; weekend traffic during summer and ski season seems to converge on the "Y" (one car passes this point each two seconds at peak times). This is normal for Tahoe City, but since the whole town is only 0.8 mile long, you will be through this mess shortly.

Most of the retail businesses in Tahoe City cater to tourists, including a large number of restaurants and bars. There is a McDonald's at the east end of town.

Tahoe City is small and makes an interesting walking tour, and you can get a walking map at the North Lake Tahoe Chamber of Commerce just east of the supermarket at the "Y."

After 0.2 miles, turn right just before the firehouse onto Commons Beach Road. Commons Beach has a free parking lot.

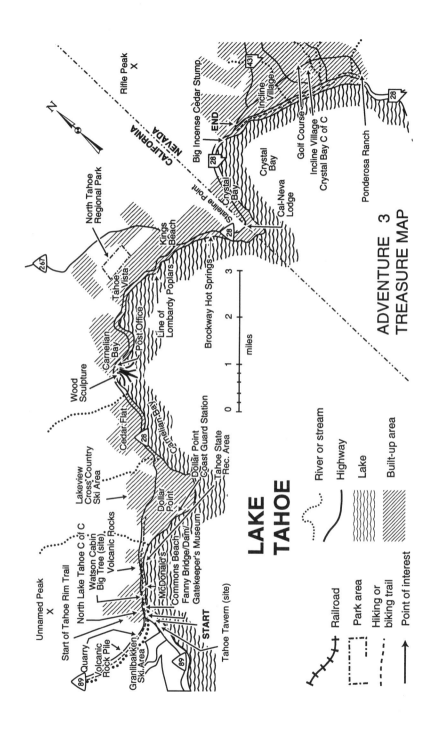

ADVENTURE 3
TREASURE MAP

Rifle Peak X

CALIFORNIA
NEVADA

N

431

Incline Village

Big Incense Cedar Stump

END

28

Crystal Bay

Golf Course
Incline Village
Crystal Bay C of C

28

Cal-Neva Lodge

Ponderosa Ranch

Stateline Point

Crystal Bay

North Tahoe Regional Park

267

Kings Beach

Tahoe Vista

28

Line of Lombardy Poplars

Post Office

Carnelian Bay

Brockway Hot Springs

miles

0   1   2   3

Wood Sculpture

Cedar Flat

28

Carnelian Bay

Dollar Point
Coast Guard Station

Tahoe State Rec. Area

LAKE TAHOE

Lakeview Cross Country Ski Area

Volcanic Rocks

Watson Cabin Big Tree (site)

North Lake Tahoe C of C

Dollar Point

McDonald's

Commons Beach

Fanny Bridge/Dam/
Gatekeeper's Museum

89

Unnamed Peak X

Start of Tahoe Rim Trail

Quarry

Volcanic Rock Pile

Granlibakken Ski Area

START

89

Tahoe Tavern (site)

River or stream

Highway

Lake

Built-up area

Railroad

Park area

Hiking or biking trail

Point of interest

If you have binoculars, get them out. The bare-topped peak directly across the Lake is Freel Peak, the highest mountain seen in these Adventures at 10,881 feet elevation (4650 feet above you), and 25 miles away. The inverted "Y" you see is in Heavenly Valley Ski Area. Towers of casinos are a little to the left of the peak. If you have binoculars, look at these tall buildings; if you don't, just pretend you can see them. The tallest is Harrah's Hotel and Casino, 19 stories tall. In front of these casinos and to the right, past Freel peak, is a series of beaches 7 miles long. However, you can't see a beach. Why? The answer is the curvature of the earth. Over 500 years ago, Christopher Columbus looked across another large body of water and saw sailing ships disappear over the horizon; this indicated to him that the earth's surface was curved. This curvature is about 1.4 feet per mile, and the beach is 20 miles away. This means that what looks to us as the other side of the lake is actually a point about 30 feet above lake level. Neat, huh?

0.4 (0.4)   There used to be a large double-trunked Jeffrey Pine tree in the middle of the road here (see sidebar for details on this tree). The log cabin on the right side of the road was built by Robert Watson in 1905. The small museum inside is open in summer, if you wish to enjoy the local history. But in the front yard there are two interesting things. The first is an Indian grinding stone with several holes; the deepest holes probably took more than one generation to grind. This grinding stone was probably used to grind two materials into flour: "pine nuts" from Singleleaf Pinyon Pine trees living in the mountains east of Carson City and acorns from California Black Oak trees living on the western slope of the Sierra Nevada. The second interesting thing is the group of five **Fremont Cottonwood** trees. These trees, undoubtedly planted when the cabin was built around 1910, average 80 feet tall and 2.8 feet in diameter at 4 1/2 feet above the ground. This will give you an idea of how quickly these trees grow. On a following page is a table comparing this non-Tahoe-native tree with Tahoe native Black Cottonwood..

****

The Tahoe City "Big Tree" — An Obituary

Until 1994 (when it died and was cut down) a big double-trunked Jeffrey Pine ruled the middle of the street 0.4 miles east of the Tahoe City "Y." This tree, already 50 feet tall when Tahoe City was founded in 1864, was almost 6 feet in diameter and over 100 feet tall at its death at age 165.

This tree is noteworthy because it was part of the soul of Tahoe City. Because of its location in the middle of the street, the California Department of Transportation (now Cal Trans) tried to cut it down when the street was paved in 1928. The Tahoe City Woman's Club circled the tree to protect it from the cutters. In 1947 citizens of the North Shore strung Christmas lights on the tree, and in the following years dubbed it "The World's Largest Christmas Tree." For 47 years it served as the focus of Christmas celebrations in Tahoe City.

Location is important for trees, and this tree was in the wrong place. The pressure of incessant traffic compacted the soil around the roots; covered with pavement, its roots could not get sufficient water, especially during the droughts of the late 1980s and early 1990s; a few out-of-contol vehicles hit the tree, and removed most of the protective bark near ground level. All of this plus the usual attacks of fungus and insects killed the tree in 1994.

Even the removal of this tree was bizarre, showing the depth of feeling about this tree: Just before it was to be cut down, people were selling "Big Tree" t-shirts; all sorts of plans were inspired as to how to dispose of the tree, including making it into a large totem pole and selling slices of it as souvenirs. And as the tree's limbs were being cut off, someone filed an injunction against this act and the city fathers met in an emergency meeting to decide what to do next. The tree was cut down and the spot ignominiously covered with a new patch of pavement.

I measured the stump. When Tahoe City was founded in 1864, each trunk was already 11 inches in diameter at 35 years old. It grew faster than any of the other trees whose stumps I have measured at Tahoe until 1928, when the highway was paved around the 104-year-old tree. Growth immediately slowed, and in the last 25 years of its life the tree only increased the diameter of each trunk 4 inches.

— Additional information in "Tales of Tahoe"

****

Feature	Fremont Cottonwood	Black Cottonwood
Leaves	Triangular, as wide Coarsely toothed	Longer than wide Finely toothed
Mature tree bark	Diamond pattern	Vertical furrows

These are the only Fremont Cottonwood trees I have seen around the Lake, although they are common along streams in the Carson Valley.

0.8 (0.4) Tahoe State Recreation area, to your right, includes a 31-unit campground. At mile 1.6 there is a swampy area on both sides of the road. The trees here (besides the ubiquitous Jeffrey Pine and White Fir) are Lodgepole Pine, Quaking Aspen and willows. All three kinds of trees do well in a moist area like this, although in some years this is too wet for Lodgepole Pines and they die (note the stumps and dead standing trees).

The rock outcrops on the left of the road 0.3 miles ahead are of volcanic rock. Note the inclination of the layered beds, up to 30 degrees toward the east. These were laid down almost flat, and the present angle testifies to the presence of the faulting here. Faulting raised the rocks on the north side of the Lake Tahoe Basin, forming a natural dam which trapped the water now in the Lake.

The lack of granitic rock outcrops from Tahoe City to Crystal Bay indicates that something else happened. Volcanic flows all along the North Shore covered the land, essentially putting the cork into the bottle that is Lake Tahoe.

1.8 (1.0) Lake Forest Drive leads 0.2 mile to a United States Coast Guard station. Think of it: if you work there, you have no gun- or drug-runners to catch, and the only Boat People are tourists.

3.5 (1.7) Fabian Road leads after about a mile to Lakeview Cross Country Ski Area, the cross country skiing area closest to the Lake. Just past it, the parking lot serves as the site of a weekly Farmer's Market, where residents get fresh vegetables from the Central Valley of California and other places (this is not a good vegetable area because the frost-free season is only about 3 months long; in fact, salad tomatoes are the only ones that ripen here). Across Highway 28 is Dollar Drive. This road goes toward a land projection called Dollar Point, the second largest land projection on the north side of the Lake.

     Dollar Point was named for shipping tycoon Robert S. Dollar, who bought much of the area in 1927. When James Lick offered a million dollars for cosntruction of an astronomical observatory, this was one site suggested. Politics set in, and by the time the dust cleared Lick Observatory was located on Mt. Hamilton, near San Jose. Dollar Point was later subdivided and now contains many upscale homes.

5.0 (1.5) The sign says "Cedar Flat" and "Pop. 200 Elevation 6480". There are two things about this. The first is that any population figure in an area with so many non-resident homeowners has to be taken with a grain of salt. The second is that Cedar Flat has no post offfice, so is it really a town?

     This brings me to another observation. I know that you have been missing seeing one thing on your trip around Lake Tahoe — mailboxes! There are essentially no mailboxes on the North Shore of Lake Tahoe because, with an average of three feet of snow cover all winter, home mail delivery would be highly time-consuming and impractical. Nearly everyone in this area has a post office box.

5.7 (0.7) Just past the curve on the right is a wood sculpture with two leopards seemingly protected inside a tree with an eagle atop it. I often see people stopping to photograph this beautiful work of art.

The tree died during the drought years, and instead of cutting it down to the ground the owner had it carved into a beautiful work of what I would call "Public Art". The sculpture, one of several along the North Shore, was done by Timeless Sculptures in Kings Beach, a few miles ahead.

About 0.2 miles ahead a post office finally appears in the little strip shopping center. Drive into this shopping center, park in front of the Carnelian Bay Post Office and stop out of your vehicle to admire the view across the road. In my opinion, this is one of the most gorgeous views from any post office anywhere.

This is a good place to compare the mountains flanking the East and West Shores of the Lake. The round-topped mountains on the left are the granitic mountains of the Carson Range. The Sierra Nevada Crest mountains on the right are also granitic, but are craggy. Valley glaciers overriding the Sierra Nevada mountains did not cover the peaks, which have been eroded by frost action along joints to present a jagged appearance.

Heavenly Valley Ski Area is in the middle background. The conical peak to its right is Mount Tallac, and the flat ridge between it and the foreground land projection of Dollar Point (made of volcanic rock) includes Rubicon Peak.

7.5 (1.8) Tahoe Vista, starting at this sign, is almost completely resort motels (starting at mile 8.0), but it is also a cultural and recreational center on the North Shore. A left turn at National Avenue (9.1) leads to North Tahoe Regional Park. During summer outdoor plays are presented there, and during winter this is a snowmobiling, sledding and cross country skiing area.

Tahoe Vista is continuous with Kings Beach, and the combined business district is 2.4 miles long. This area serves a dual purpose; although tourism is the main business, this is also the bedroom community for many of the people working in the tourism industry on the North Shore.

9.3 (1.8) As you round the curve to the left, the most striking feature is a line of trees whose branches seem to be pointing straight upward. These are **Lombardy Poplar**, a cultivated variety of Black Poplar (native to Europe and western Asia). Because of its shape, Lombardy Poplar is effective as a windbreak as well as an ornamental tree. It is widely planted in the United States, and is found in a number of places around the Lake. Its main drawback is that it is a poplar, and poplar roots tend to go after water and sewer lines. In autumn, its leaves are a beautiful yellow color.

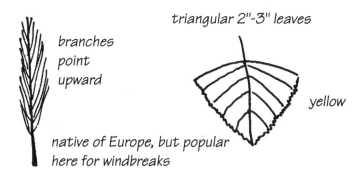

branches
point
upward

triangular 2"-3" leaves

yellow

native of Europe, but popular
here for windbreaks

Lombardy Poplar

(1.1) At the end of the business district, just before the highway turns right and uphill, is a sign for Brockway Springs Condominiums. The condominium management pipes hot spring water into the various condos.

For me, the significance of these hot springs (the only ones along the side of Lake Tahoe) is that volcanic activity is still present in the Lake Tahoe Basin.

11.2 (1.2) To the right of the State of Nevada sign is a road leading to Cal-Neva Lodge, which makes an interesting few-minute visit. Built in 1927 as a guest house for prospective real estate investors, this place straddling the California-Nevada state line was a natural for a casino when Nevada re-legalized gambling in 1931.

Frank Sinatra bought 50 percent of the hotel-casino in 1962, but his gaming license was terminated because it was rumored that famous Mafioso Sam Giancana was staying there; Sinatra soon sold out.

The Cal-Neva Lodge has another claim to fame: it is one of the most popular places to get married at Tahoe. 2800 marriages take place there annually, many of them at a gazebo on the Lake side of the hotel. This gazebo is on a concrete pad complete with a painted white line for the bridal march; the pad can seat 300 people. And with Tahoe's 307 sunny days a year, it's a good "bet" that the marriage will be celebrated in sunshine.

Look at the trees landscaped trees in front of the building. There are many non-native species; the ones I noticed are ash trees and a 40-foot Canyon Live Oak. Although this tree is extremely common in the Sierra Nevada, this is above its normal range. Except for a grove of trees on the Vikingsholm hike (see Adventure 7 for a sketch), this is the only Canyon Live Oak I have seen at Tahoe.

There are four other casinos along the highway, which is now renamed Nevada 28. The village here is Crystal Bay, Nevada; it has its own post office, but it is administered jointly with Incline Village, 1.5 miles ahead. This interesting area will be described in more detail in Adventure 4, a road log from Incline Village to the South Lake Tahoe "Y."

The Cal-Neva Lodge is on a land projection called Stateline Point. About 2000 feet east of Stateline Point, the water depth is 1200 feet. This is another place where faulting caused steep water bottom topography.

12.0 (0.8) Between the trees adjoining the highway you may see a rock formation which looks like a rifle sight. This is Rifle Peak. Note that the trees near the top of this and other nearby mountains (at about 9000 feet elevation, or 2800 feet above us) seem to be shorter and sparser.

The climate is much harsher there than here, and the forest cannot support many trees.

13.4 (1.4)   About 50 feet from the left edge of the highway and about 200 feet before the driveway for the second set of Lakeside condominiums, is a huge Incense Cedar stump, the oldest one I have seen in the Lake Tahoe Basin with 650 annual rings.

14.2 (0.8)   The intersection of Nevada 431 and Nevada 28 marks the end of this Adventure and the start of Adventure 4 (the trip from Incline Village to the South Lake Tahoe "Y") and Adventure 5 (the trip to Reno). About a half mile ahead is the start of the Incline Village business district.

ADVENTURE 4

Incline Village to South Lake Tahoe

This Adventure is a segment of the drive around Lake Tahoe (see the map in the Foreword for orientation). It starts at the intersection of Nevada 431 (Mount Rose Highway) and Nevada 28. It goes along Nevada 28 and U.S. 50 on the East Shore of Lake Tahoe to the California-Nevada state line, and then across the South Shore of Lake Tahoe to the South Lake Tahoe "Y."

Driving time around this section of the Lake is about one hour. However, there are many places for stopping, and depending on the time spent on these, this Adventure will take up to about 4 hours.

As in the other Adventures with road logs, there are two sets of numbers at the left side of the page. The number outside the parentheses is mileage from the start of the Adventure; the number inside the parentheses is the distance between notations.

Appendix A gives demographics for communities along this Adventure.

0.5 (0.5)   The business district of Incline Village is 1.3 miles long and has three traffic lights. Incline Village and Crystal Bay are administered jointly, and total some 7,000 people. Curiously, only 46 percent of the residences are owner-occupied; the rest are second homes, owned primarily by residents of the San Francisco Bay Area, and visited on weekends and summertime.

1.5 (1.0)   On the left is one of the three golf courses fronting the main highways around Lake Tahoe. This course was designed by the noted Robert Tent Jones, Jr. Across the highway is the Incline Village-Crystal Bay Chamber of Commerce. Country Club Boulevard, at the traffic light, leads to Diamond Peak Ski Area, which is one of three ski areas situated at the side of the Lake. Diamond Peak Ski Area was designed as part of the Incline planned community, a local skiing area for Incline Village residents. See the sidebar for more information about Incline Village.

****

Incline Village

Now an upscale residential community, Incline Village originally was a Washoe Indian village. In 1879 a lumber mill was built here by the Sierra Nevada Wood and Lumber Company. Logs were brought not only from local forests but by barge from the southern end of the Lake. The company built an incline railway 4000 feet long to transport logs 1400 feet vertically to a tunnel built by a water company. They built a V-shaped flume inside the water tunnel, and slid the logs into the Carson Valley.

By the time the mill closed in 1893, the mines were just about shut down and the forest around Incline was just about gone. Since the land was useless to lumber companies, they sold it. Over a period of years George Whittell bought 35,000 acres of East Shore land, and built a mansion on it a few miles south of town.

As the 1950s waned, there was a land boom at the Lake. A company named Crystal Bay Development Company bought 9000 acres from Whittell from the California state line to near the millsite, and developed one of only two planned communities at Lake Tahoe. This community has its own skiing area and a golf course designed by Robert Trent Jones Jr. There are now about 6000 housing units in town.

Incline Village and Crystal Bay are parts of this planned community, which is governed by Incline Village General Improvement District (IVGID).

— Additional information in "Tahoe: An Environmental History" and "Sawdust Trails in the Truckee Basin"

****

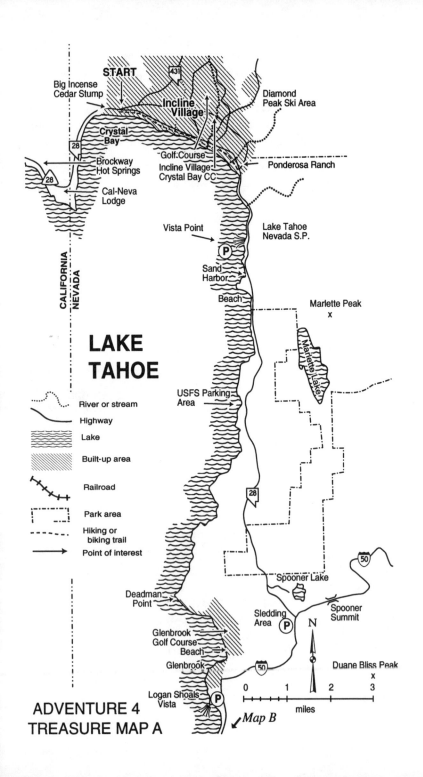

START

Big Incense
Cedar Stump

431

Incline
Village

Diamond
Peak Ski Area

Crystal
Bay

28

N

Brockway
Hot Springs

Golf Course

Incline Village
Crystal Bay CC

Ponderosa Ranch

28

Cal-Neva
Lodge

Vista Point

Lake Tahoe
Nevada S.P.

P

CALIFORNIA
NEVADA

Sand
Harbor

Beach

Marlette Peak
x

LAKE
TAHOE

Marlette Lake

River or stream

Highway

Lake

Built-up area

USFS Parking
Area

Railroad

Park area

Hiking or
biking trail

Point of interest

28

I-50

Spooner Lake

Deadman
Point

Sledding
Area

P

Spooner
Summit

N

Glenbrook
Golf Course

Beach

Glenbrook

50

Logan Shoals
Vista

P

Duane Bliss Peak
x

0   1   2   3

miles

Map B

ADVENTURE 4
TREASURE MAP A

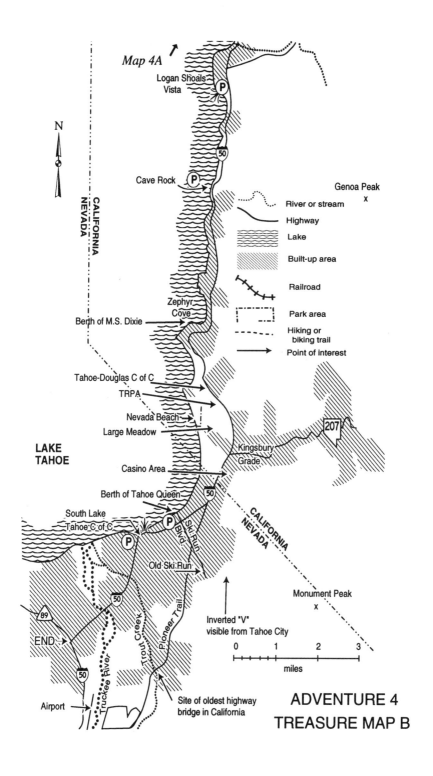

Map 4A

Logan Shoals
Vista

P

50

Cave Rock P

N

CALIFORNIA
NEVADA

Genoa Peak
x

River or stream
Highway
Lake
Built-up area
Railroad
Park area
Hiking or
biking trail
Point of interest

Zephyr
Cove
Berth of M.S. Dixie

Tahoe-Douglas C of C
TRPA
Nevada Beach
Large Meadow

LAKE
TAHOE

207

Kingsbury
Grade

Casino Area

Berth of Tahoe Queen

50

South Lake
Tahoe C of C

P

P

Ski Run Blvd

CALIFORNIA
NEVADA

Old Ski Run

89

50

Truckee River

Trout Creek

Pioneer Trail

Monument Peak
x

Inverted "V"
visible from Tahoe City

0   1   2   3

miles

END

Airport

50

Site of oldest highway
bridge in California

ADVENTURE 4
TREASURE MAP B

2.9 (1.4) This is the entrance to the Ponderosa Ranch, a spinoff of the TV show "Bonanza." Almost all exterior scenes from the first Bonanza series (from 1958 to 1973) were filmed in this area, and catering and other support functions for the production company were a major business in town. Interior scenes from the ranch house were filmed in Hollywood until 1967, when the ranch house replica above you on the hill was built. People from all over the world have seen the Bonanza series, and many Ponderosa Ranch visitors come from other countries; this "theme park" has about 200,000 visitors per year.

Why is this ranch called the "Ponderosa" when most of the pines here are Jeffreys? First of all, would you rather name your ranch "The Jeffrey" or "The Ponderosa?" Second, there are a few Ponderosas at the Lake, including some in the parking lot.

3.7 (0.8) (The Lake Tahoe Nevada State Park sign) This park, first conceived in the 1920s, contains 13,000 acres; the next three miles of Lake frontage are in the Park. This park fulfilled Nevada's desire to preserve for the future some of the area adjacent to Lake Tahoe shoreline.

4.9 (1.2) Pull off into the parking lot on the right side of the road, a good spot for a Lake vista. On the right is a flat-topped range of granitic mountains which includes Rifle Peak (Adventure 3). Beneath the mountains is Incline Village. The houses high on the hill are up to 1400 feet above Lake level.

The middle-ground land projection is Stateline Point (made of volcanic rock), and the building on it is Cal-Neva Lodge. The two round-topped mountains to the left are Mount Pluto and Mount Watson, two volcanoes through which much volcanic material flowed into the region. To the left behind them are the glaciated granitic peaks of the Sierra Nevada Crest, including the mountains around Squaw Valley and Alpine Meadows Ski Areas.

Here's a clue about local geology: if the mountain is low and forested, it's made of volcanic rock; if its peak is jagged and bare of trees it's made of granitic rock.

Left of the two volcanoes is Tahoe City and the Truckee River Valley. The skiing area further left is Ski Homewood, which is on the route of Adventure 2. Left of it the flat-topped range includes Rubicon Peak, with Emerald Bay and Mount Tallac further left.

Shrubs present alongside the many trails leading down to the edge of the water include Manzanita and **Huckleberry Oak** (see Adventure 7 for sketches and descriptions), but there are also shrubs of another group of plants. These plants (**Basin Sagebrush, Bitterbrush** and **Rabbit Brush**) are typical of the desert areas east of the Carson Range above you, but this is a good place to see them. Basin Sagebrush — evergreen, gray-green, aromatic and with three-lobed leaves, is the most widespread and best known shrub of western deserts. Although it harbors a wide assortment of reptiles, insects, birds and mammals, it is unpalatable to browsing animals. More palatable is Bitterbrush, which loses its leaves in winter. Rabbit Brush does not have the twisted, many-twigged branches of the other two species but instead looks like a "weed," complete with colorful yellow masses of blossoms in late summer and fall. It has an unpleasant smell, which probably accoubts for its species name, "nauseosus."

Down by the Lake are huge boulders. Many rocks at Tahoe are rounded by glaciers or streams; but this side of the Lake had little glaciation, and these boulders are too large to be carried by streams. So what is their origin? The sidebar on a later page tells how these rocks got rounded.

As you descend, you may see the typical dark blue water of Lake Tahoe with patches of emerald-green water. The water is not actually blue; it reflects the colors of the sky at a particular moment.

leaves are silvery gray,
stay on tree all winter,
smell like sage

1"
leaves

yellow-green 6"-12" flower
spikes with tiny flowers

bloom July to November

Basin Sagebrush

1/2"
leaves

leaf shape like Basin
Sagebrush, bark dark
green, leaves fall off

1/2"-1"
flowers

smells like resin

Bitterbrush

looks like a "weed"
rather than a shrub

usually found with Bitterbrush
and Basin Sagebrush

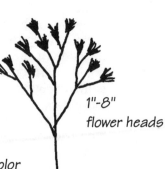

1"-8"
flower heads

yellow flowers brighten desert
highways with summer and fall color

Rabbit Brush

A typical summer day's colors are white to pink at sunrise, deepening into dark grayish blue in the afternoon, and fading into white with a purplish cast at twilight. The emerald green color? Large boulders near the Lake surface have a slimy covering of algae, and reflect the sky color; but sandy areas of the bottom do not have algae clinging to them, and are shallow enough that sunlight reflects off the nearly white sand grains; the result is the wonderful emerald green color reminis-cent of the Caribbean.

5.8 (0.9) Sand Harbor Beach, to the right, has not only been rated the "best place to watch the sunset from" at the Lake; it is also the site of the Annual Shakespeare Festival in Late July. Theatergoers set lawn chairs, food, wine and blankets on the sand near the beach; the atmosphere is like that of a small-town parade. And the plays are well-done.

At the water's edge on the next point of land is a house. This house, on private property, is the former residence of George Whittell, the man who once owned the land on which both Lake Tahoe Nevada State Park and Incline Village sit. If you want to buy the house and grounds, they are for sale. Price? $60 million.

8.0 (2.2) To the left and right is a picnic area with limited parking operated by the U.S. Forest Service; 0.4 miles further, past the sign saying "Carson City Rural Area" and among all the "No Parking" signs, is the entrance for a large parking area. It has an interpretative sign, and trails down to the Lake.

You may notice that virtually all the forest trees are Jeffrey Pine, with only a few White Firs and Incense Cedars. Either this area is a little too dry for White Fir or, when the forests were logged, fewer White Firs were left standing than on the West Shore.

12.4 (4.4) The meadow area left of the highway just past the Douglas County Line signals that you are close to the turnoff for Spooner Lake. This area, a good picnic area

****

Weathering Rounds Rocks at Lake Tahoe

Many of the rocks in this area are rounded; but there was no glacial sandpapering and abrasion as at Emerald Bay (there was little glaciation on this side of the Lake), nor was there wave action like that at Hurricane Bay, nor are there any streams near here. So what happened?

The forces which lifted the magnificent mountains at Tahoe miles above where they were formed were so powerful that they also cracked the rock. These cracks, called "joints," are common all over the mountains; this outcrop has a number of straight joints. Note that they intersect.

The granite making up the rocks has two primary mineral components. Quartz, the mineral which makes up many beautiful beach sands, is chemically very stable; feldspar, the other mineral, is chemically unstable. In the presence of water, feldspar changes chemically to clay over a period of many, many years. Feldspar is a strong material, but clay is not. It may wash out of the rock, leaving the quartz and remaining feldspar grains with no support; also, volume changes in the chemical reactions from feldspar to clay create stresses in the original rock. The granite here originally had no holes for the water to enter and change the feldspar, so the water had to penetrate crystal by crystal — except at the joints, where it could move easily. Chemical processes changed feldspar into clay all along the straight intersecting joints. Eventually the rock, completely detached from its neighbors, tumbled downhill.

For some reason, the chemical weathering seems to be stronger at the joint intersections, so there is quicker weathering there. The net result is that the rock ends up rounded.

— Additional information in books on geology

****

and starting place for hikes to Marlette Lake to the north, is also an area of groomed cross country skiing. Like many other local lakes, this lake was dammed so that flow from it could be regulated.

13.4 (1.0) Take the right lane leading to U.S. 50 and South Lake Tahoe. The parking area to the right is one of two free sledding areas near the Lake; the other is just south of Tahoe City on U.S. 89.

Highway 50, from Carson City (about 13 miles east of here) to Placerville, California (about 75 miles west of here) marks one of the favorite routes of nineteenth century travelers.

14.2 (0.8) The sign: "Trooper Gary Gifford Memorial Highway" perhaps indicates a turning point in United States history. In 1975, this Nevada Highway Patrolman stopped a car near Cave Rock and was killed by the occupants, one of the first such incidents in U.S. history. The state decided to name this part of U.S. 50 in his honor. Sadly, today this type of event is too common.

15.2 (1.0) To the right is a good view of a golf course and sandy beach from 400 feet above. One mile further, at 16.2, is the turnoff for Glenbrook, the site of the one of the largest lumber mills in the Truckee River Basin. The roadside interpretative sign gives some information about Glenbrook.

17.8 (2.6) The sign indicates that the Logan Shoal Vista Point is just ahead on the right. This is a good vista point for this area of the Lake. Two prominent features visible from here are the 1100-foot-high landslide scar at Emerald Bay, easily seen though about 12 miles away; and the conical Mt. Tallac, at 9375 feet one of the tallest mountains on the west side of the Lake Tahoe Basin, and the site of the Tallac Cross (which you can see from here in fall and spring). The distant peaks on the right are above Squaw Valley, about 20 miles away; if you travel this road on a clear night, you can see the lights of the Squaw Valley High Camp. Most of the shrubs here are Manzanita.

18.9 (1.1) The right tunnel through Cave Rock was built in 1931 to replace an auto road to the right of the highway. Just past the tunnel, between the traffic lanes, you can park to explore this area. Cross the road carefully — oncoming vehicles cannot see you until they exit the tunnel — and walk back along the old road, a replacement for an old Indian trail. On the north side of Cave Rock the road disappears; the sheer drop necessitated a terrifying traverse across a trestle. This rock, a volcanic neck like Eagle Rock south of Tahoe City (Adventure 2), contained a cave which, according to the story you choose to believe, was either an Indian shelter, a sacred/haunted place, or a fortress. Whichever it was, the cave was essentially destroyed when the rock was tunneled. Past Cave Rock, civilization (housing) starts once again; the first traffic light in 20 miles is at Zephyr Cove. A right turn brings you to the berth for the paddlewheeler steamer MS Dixie II, which features dinner cruises and daily excursions to Emerald Bay and Glenbrook.

23.2 (4.3) The meadow on the right side of the road right after the sign for Marla Bay may look familiar; it was used for the opening sequence of each Bonanza TV show. If you want to check this out, drive by slowly; there is no place to park here.

24.1 (0.9) Past the conical round hill on the right (appropriately named Round Hill), on the left in the shopping center before the traffic light at Elks Point Road, is the Tahoe-Douglas Chamber of Commerce. A right on Elks Point Road leads to Nevada Beach, site of the first campground on the Nevada side of the Lake; but it also leads to the headquarters of the Tahoe Regional Planning Agency (TRPA), an agency with the unenviable task of regulating growth in the Lake Tahoe Basin (see sidebar for more details).

****

The Tahoe Regional Planning Agency (TRPA)

When Tahoe was first settled by white men in the 1860s, the few inhabitants did not have much impact on this great natural resource. But as time went on many people visited this fabulous place, and wealthy people built summer houses here. With increasingly good transportation, more people came, both for tourism and for residence.

By the 1960s, the tourist population on peak summer weekends had swelled to over 120,000 and part of the natural beauty of Tahoe — the clear, clean river and Lake water and the clear skies — was endangered by the stress of so many people. The beautiful mountain peaks became hazy because of air pollution, the legendary clarity of the Lake was decreasing because of algal growth, and new construction was eroding topsoil that took thousands of years to develop. And there were predictions of 800,000 residents within 20 years. Unrestrained growth had stressed the environment and beauty-lovers were quite worried.

Here were two typical components of contemporary American society — the wish to preserve the environment and the need for commerce. At their most extreme, absentee landowners, most of whom were financially secure, wanted to preserve the environment at any financial cost, and local businessmen wanted to make a buck at any environmental cost. Clearly, somethng had to be done; in this context the TRPA was born.

The TRPA regulates construction, remodeling, tree removal and population growth in the Lake Tahoe Basin. This is an unenviable task, because no mater what they decide, someone whose interests are not being served is mad at them.

— Additional information in "Tahoe: An Environmental History"

****

25.4 (0.8) The traffic light before the big casinos signals the intersection of U.S. 50 and Nevada 207, known locally as "Kingsbury Grade." In the 1860s, this road was important in two respects. First, it was one the early routes over this part of the Sierra Nevada; toll road operators charged farmers seeking fertile California valleys for passage on the way west, and charged would-be miners for passage on the way east.

Second, another group charging across Kingsbury Grade were the Pony Express riders. This operation, romanticized in Western history with images of sweating horses with tongues hanging out and wide-eyed dusty riders, actually only operated from 1860 to 1861, when the Civil War broke out and the telegraph made the Pony Express obsolete. Nevertheless, one of the many changes of mounts occurred near this intersection. The Pony Express is commemorated with a bronze statue in front of Harrah's Casino.

****

Gambling

In the American West of the nineteenth century, gambling ran rampant. Nevada legalized it in 1869, five years after statehood. But during the Progressive Era in 1910, anti-gambling forces prevailed and the Nevada Legislature made gambling illegal. The result was that state revenue decreased dramatically but there was almost no effect on gambling. After more than twenty years, Nevada legalized gambling again in 1931.

Gambling came to Tahoe in the 1930s, but it didn't take over until after World War II, when Harvey Gross established Harvey's. William Harrah established Harrah's Tahoe in 1955. Today there are two other major casinos on the South Shore and several smaller ones on the North Shore. It is hard to estimate gambling revenue, but it is certainly in the billions of dollars annually, and it forms the backbone of the South Tahoe economy.

****

26.1 (0.7) The change in architecture from vertical to horizontal marks the California-Nevada state line. A half mile further is Pioneer Trail, now just a city street but in the nineteenth century one of the main byways west, the route of tens of thousands of people.

27.4 (1.3) Ski Run Boulevard is named after an informal straight downhill skiing run in the middle of South Lake Tahoe. In 1947 two rope tows, a warming hut and floodlights (for night skiing) were added, and the area became locally known as the Bijou Park Skiway. In the mid-1950s, the skiing run was abandoned, paved, and named Ski Run Blvd.

    To the right is the berth for the Tahoe Queen, another paddlewheeler steamer. Mainly used for day cruises to Emerald Bay and dinner dance cruises on the Lake, it also provides a daily ski shuttle to the North Shore in winter, a six-hour round trip across twenty miles of Lake Tahoe for a day of skiing may seem strange; but the view is awesome, and there is no other public transportation from the South Shore to the North Shore.

    Why is there no other public transportation between North Tahoe and South Tahoe? I can think of two good reasons: first, in winter U.S. 89 is frequently closed by snow, and if it is open travel may be slowed by bad road conditions; although Nevada 28 and U.S. 50 rarely close, they too are plagued by frequent winter snowstorms.

    Second, each shore is self-contained. Tourists on the South Shore have Heavenly Valley Ski Area (reached by driving uphill on Ski Run Boulevard for about five minutes), a variety of hiking and biking trails nearby, sandy or rocky beaches, and the Stateline casinos; tourists on the North Shore have ski areas within a few minute drive of wherever they are staying, a variety of hiking and biking trails nearby, sandy or rocky beaches, and and the Crystal Bay casinos. Shopping, dining and services are similar for residents on each shore. So neither group needs to go to the other shore.

Fortunately, there is the Tahoe Queen, and the scenic highways you are traveling, to bring both shores together.

This provinciality breeds antipathy and contempt: South Shore residents think that North Shore people are rich snobs, and North Shore residents think of the South Shore as a combination of casinos and slums. There may be a grain of truth in these perceptions, but just a grain of truth.

The mountain you see as you continue toward the end of this Adventure is Mount Tallac, at 9735 feet arguably the tallest mountain rising from the Lake shore.

28.2 (0.8) This is the start of the free quarter-mile-long Regan Beach, which provides a good vista of the northern half of the Lake. There is some parking on the right at the traffic light for Lakeview Avenue, and beach parking about one half mile right on Lakeview Avenue.

The beach has both sand and mud, and there are a lot of water-loving plants on the beach. The sand and mud both come from the Upper Truckee River and Trout Creek (the largest streams draining into the Lake), which form a delta into the Lake about a mile west of here. Because there is so much sediment conimg into the Lake here, the Lake water offshore is sandy brown. Farther from the beach, the water is the typical Tahoe Blue. Starting from the right side of the beach, the conical hill is Round Hill. In back of Round Hill and the other low hills is the Carson Range. The jagged peak in the right center distance is Mount Rose, some 20 miles distant. The two rounded peaks at center are Mount Pluto and Mount Watson. Continuing leeft, you can see the mountains of the Sierra Nevada Crest. Rubicon Peak is the rocky-toopped peak at the right of the highest set of mountains. The depression left of these mountains is Emerald Bay. Mount Tallac is out of sight to the left.

On the left side of the highway, just past the light, is the Lake Tahoe Museum, as well as the South Lake Tahoe Chamber of Commerce.

29.3 (1.1) Bridges here and at 30.3 mark the crossing of the highway over Trout Creek and the Upper Truckee River. These two streams drain almost 100 square miles, and provide a third of the water going into the Lake. Incidentally, the forerunner of the culvert over Trout Creek at Pioneer Trail, about two miles south of here, was the first highway bridge built in California, in 1898.

30.7 (1.4) A right turn on Tahoe Keys Blvd. leads to the Tahoe Keys Marina, a massive subdivision on the marshland of the Upper Truckee River Delta. Several hundred homeowners can berth boats in back of their homes in the 150-foot-wide dredged lagoons 14 feet deep. With present-day TRPA rules, this subdivision could not have been built because it is on easily-erodible land, and massive erosion would endanger the esthetic beauty of the Lake, claimed to have the third-clearest water of any lake in the world.

31.3 (0.6) The South Lake Tahoe "Y" is the end of this Adventure.

ADVENTURE 5

A Trip to Reno

This Adventure has some tree species not normally seen in highway routes around Lake Tahoe. It starts at the intersection of Nevada 28 and Nevada 431 (Mount Rose Highway), which is also the starting point and ending pont of Adventures 4 and 3 respectively (see the map in the Foreword for orientation). Mount Rose Highway is kept open even in winter except during heavy snowstorms. There are two options: the first is to enjoy the beautiful drive on Nevada 431 to Mount Rose Summit and retrace your steps, for an Adventure of an hour or two, and you can see a number of new tree species.

The second is to continue on a full-day trip to Reno via U.S. 395, travelling Interstate 80 to Truckee, then on California 89 to the Tahoe City "Y," where the Adventure ends at the starting and ending points for Adventures 3 and 2 respectively.

The advantage of the first option is that it is shorter and can be an interesting addition to the route around the Lake covered in Adventures 2 through 4. The advantage of the second option is thatyou can experiencethe contrast between the forested Lake Tahoe Basin and the non-forested High Desert, the spectacular Truckee River Canyon and the town of Truckee.

The second option also includes opportunities for exploring thebeautiful arboretum that is Idlewild Park (Adventure 6; allow two hours), Side Trip B to examine the rare Washoe Pine (a half hour) and Side Trip C to the Donner Pass area (two hours).

As in the other Adventures with road logs, there are two sets of numbers at the left side of the page. The number outside the parentheses is mileage from the start of the Adventure; the number inside the parentheses is the distance between notations.

Appendix A gives the demographics for some towns along this Adventure.

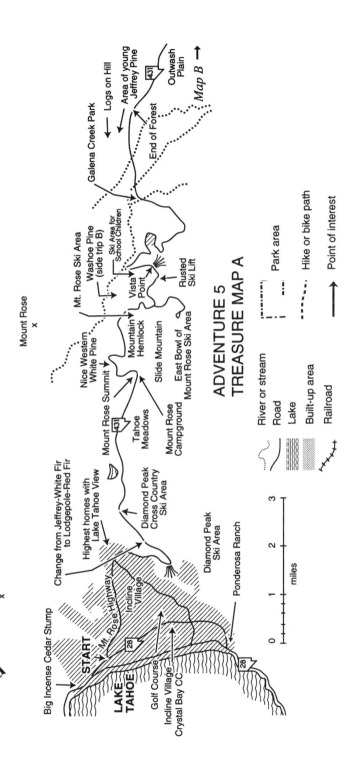

ADVENTURE 5
TREASURE MAP A

Rifle Peak
x

Mount Rose
x

Big Incense Cedar Stump

START

LAKE TAHOE

Change from Jeffrey-White Fir to Lodgepole-Red Fir

Highest homes with Lake Tahoe View

Mt. Rose Highway

Incline Village

Golf Course

Incline Village Crystal Bay CC

28

Diamond Peak Cross Country Ski Area

Diamond Peak Ski Area

Ponderosa Ranch

28

Nice Western White Pine

Mount Rose Summit

431

Tahoe Meadows

Mount Rose Campground

Mountain Hemlock

Slide Mountain

East Bowl of Mount Rose Ski Area

Mt. Rose Ski Area

Washoe Pine (side trip B)

Vista Point

Ski Area for School Children

Rusted Ski Lift

Galena Creek Park

Logs on Hill

Area of young Jeffrey Pine

End of Forest

431

Outwash Plain

Map B →

miles
0   1   2   3

River or stream
Road
Lake
Built-up area
Railroad

Park area
Hike or bike path
→ Point of interest

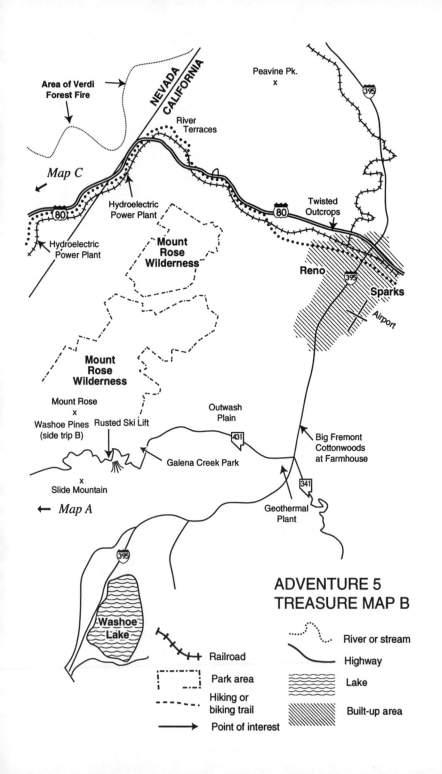

Area of Verdi Forest Fire

NEVADA
CALIFORNIA

Peavine Pk.
x

395

River Terraces

Map C

80

Hydroelectric Power Plant

Hydroelectric Power Plant

80

Twisted Outcrops

Mount Rose Wilderness

Reno

395

Sparks

Airport

Mount Rose Wilderness

Mount Rose
x
Washoe Pines
(side trip B)

Rusted Ski Lift

Outwash Plain

431

Big Fremont Cottonwoods at Farmhouse

Galena Creek Park

341

x
Slide Mountain

← *Map A*

Geothermal Plant

395

Washoe Lake

ADVENTURE 5
TREASURE MAP B

┼──┼──┼──┼ Railroad

─ · ─ · ─ Park area

─ ─ ─ ─ Hiking or biking trail

────→ Point of interest

········· River or stream

───── Highway

〰〰〰 Lake

▨▨▨ Built-up area

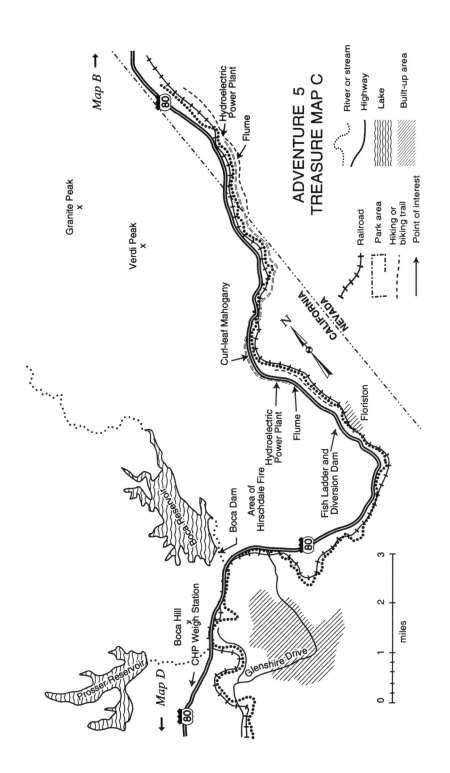

ADVENTURE 5
TREASURE MAP C

River or stream
Highway
Lake
Built-up area

Railroad
Park area
Hiking or biking trail
Point of interest

Map B →

Granite Peak
x

Verdi Peak
x

Hydroelectric
Power Plant
Flume

Curl-leaf Mahogany

Hydroelectric Power Plant
Flume

Area of
Hirschdale Fire

Fish Ladder and
Diversion Dam

Floriston

CALIFORNIA
NEVADA

N

Boca Dam

Boca
Reservoir

Boca Hill
CHP Weigh Station
x

Prosser Reservoir

Map D
↓

Glenshire Drive

0   1   2   3
miles

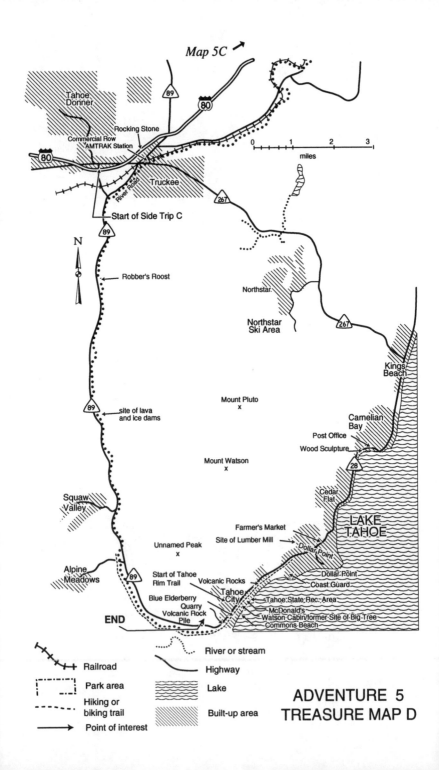

Map 5C

Tahoe
Donner

Commercial Row
AMTRAK Station

Rocking Stone

89   80

80

0   1   2   3
miles

River Road

Truckee

267

Start of Side Trip C

N

89

Robber's Roost

Northstar

Northstar
Ski Area

267

Kings
Beach

89

site of lava
and ice dams

Mount Pluto
x

Carnelian
Bay

Post Office

Wood Sculpture

28

Mount Watson
x

Cedar
Flat

Squaw
Valley

LAKE
TAHOE

Farmer's Market

Site of Lumber Mill

Dollar Point

Unnamed Peak
x

Alpine
Meadows

89

Start of Tahoe
Rim Trail

Volcanic Rocks

Dollar Point

Coast Guard

Tahoe
City

Blue Elderberry
Quarry

Tahoe State Rec. Area

McDonald's

END

Volcanic Rock
Pile

Watson Cabin/former Site of Big Tree

Commons Beach

Railroad

River or stream

Park area

Highway

Hiking or
biking trail

Lake

Point of interest

Built-up area

ADVENTURE 5
TREASURE MAP D

Why does the vegetation change so drastically (as we shall see) from Incline Village to Reno? Not only does the road go from an elevation of around 6250 feet in Incline Village to 8911 feet at Mount Rose Summit to around 4450 feet in Reno, but the mean annual precipitation goes from 21 inches in Incline Village to 35 inches at Mount Rose Summit to seven inches in Reno. In the Sierra Nevada, both elevation and precipitation are important in determining the types of trees found.

0.0 (0.0) As you ascend the rather steep highway, notice two things. First, most of the year there are bicyclists speeding down this road at speeds about 40 miles an hour. They are doing this because they are taking some time back from Mother Nature (if they started at Lake level and went to Mount Rose Summit, they had to climb 2700 feet; if they started in the Carson Valley, they had to climb 4500 feet). I am a bicyclist, and I'd do it too.

Second, the houses are blended, almost camouflaged, into the woods. This is typical of Incline Village. Apollo Way, the last residential street for 16 miles, is the highest street with a view of the Lake (at 7600 feet elevation, or almost 1400 feet above Lake level).

3.7 (3.7) On the right at the apex of the sweeping turn to the left is what has been voted the most beautiful view in the whole north half of the Lake Tahoe Basin (peobably because it is 1400 feet above the Lake and there is a 3D perspective. Let's stop and check it out.

Theleftmost mountain on the ridge to the right is Rifle Peak. To its left are the rounded peaks of the volcanoes Mount Pluto and Mount Watson. To their left is KT-22, a peak overlooking Squaw Valley Ski Area. The large land projection and the building on it are Stateline Point and the Cal-Neva Lodge; behind them the land projectionis Dollar Point. The rounded canyon directly behind the Cal-Neva Lodge is Blackwood Canyon, which has the U-shape typical of glacial valleys, as do the next two canyons to the left. Left of these is a ridge with Rubicon Peak as the jagged-topped mountain; behind the ridge is the Sierra Nevada Crest, with Dick's Peak the tallest peak on that edge of the Lake Tahoe Basin. The valley left of this ridge contains Emerald Bay, and left of that is Mount Tallac.

Below us is Incline Village. the tallest building is the Hyatt Regency Lake Tahoe, sharing with the Cal-Neva Lodge the distinction of being the tallest structure on the North Shore.

The distant land projection with the mountain on it is Deadman Point, and directly behind it the jagged peaks are at the southern boundary of the Lake Tahoe Basin some 30 miles away. The tallest mountain at left center is Freel Peak. The land projection between us and Deadman Point is Sand Point, and the mountain directly above (to the left) of it is Marlette Peak. On the left edge of opurview are some skiing runs for Diamond Peak Ski Area.

4.7 (1.0) At this elevation (7800 feet), **Lodgepole Pine** and **Red Fir** have replaced Jeffrey Pine and White Fir as the predominant trees. For the next nine miles, there are almost no trees of the latter species. Sketches on the next page show how to distinguish between the two fir species and to identify Lodgepole Pine.

This is the boundary between the Yellow Pine Belt (also called the Transition Zone) and the Lodgepole Pine-Red Fir Belt (also called the Canadian Zone). The reason there are different trees is complex, but it is at least partly because the Lodgepole and Red Fir can stand a little lower average winter temperature.

The Lodgepole Pine-Red Fir Belt receives the greatest amount of precipitation in the Sierra Nevada, but it also gets the most lightning strikes of any belt. Since Red Fir is typically the tallest tree of this belt, it gets the bulk of these strikes. Many of the Red Firs around you have characteristic multiple tops; lightning has killed the leader of these trees, and each tree had to grow new tops via the horizontal branches near its top.

Feature	White Fir	Red Fir
bark of mature tree	gray	reddish brown
pure stands?	almost never	common
needles	twist at base, go away from twig	no twist at base, go along twig

Red Fir vs. White Fir

"popcorn" bark

some 2" cones stay
on branch for years

1"-2" needles

sometimes disease causes
swelling of branches

Lodgepole Pine

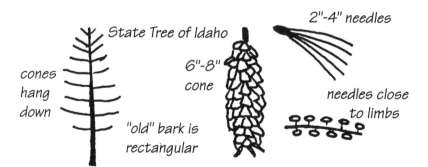

State Tree of Idaho

cones
hang
down

6"-8"
cone

"old" bark is
rectangular

2"-4" needles

needles close
to limbs

Western White Pine

Many of the Red Fir trees have yellow growths on their bark. This organism is **Staghorn Lichen**, a symbiotic combination of a fungus and a colony of microscopic one-celled algae. Although Staghorn Lichen grows on many tree species, it is found on a great percentage of Red Fir trunks. This slow-growing lichen is resistant to cold, drought and direct sunlight. Notice that it does not reach the ground. The lower limit of Staghorn Lichen on trees is a good indication of the snowpack depth during winter (check this out by comparing base of lichen growth in both high and low areas).

Where Red Fir dominates a stand there are essentially no shrubs or flowers underneath it. A Red Fir's shade is so dense that it shades out almost other plants, including its own seedlings.

5.2 (0.5) Past the sign for the Diamond Peak Cross Country Ski Area, look to the right for pine trees different from Lodgepole Pine. Old trees of this species have a rectangular or hexagonal bark pattern (as opposed to the "popcorn" bark pattern of mature to old Lodgepole Pines), and six-inch cones droop from branches most of the year. These are **Western White Pine** trees (see the sketch on the next page), with five needles in a cluster as opposed to Lodgepole Pine's two. Western White Pine is found in scattered groves, and rarely dominates a stand.

Wait a minute, you say. How do I know I'm not looking at Sugar Pine (of which there are many trees at Lake level)? Good question: Like Western White Pine, Sugar Pine has five needles per bundle, and its upper branches are also apparently flung out from the trunk with needles clustered very close to the branches. But Sugar Pines are rarely found above 7000 feet, and Western White Pines are almost never seen below 7000 feet; and Sugar Pine cones are much larger, commonly a foot long. Adventure 2 has a description of Sugar Pine.

As you travel up the highway, keep looking for Western White Pines among the Lodgepole Pines.

6.7 (1.5) The open area with almost no trees is locally called "Tahoe Meadows". It teems with families during the winter, when there is plenty of snow and few trees to obstruct sleds. It is also a popular area for cross country skiers and snowmobilers. In the summer many families walk through the meadow because of its beautiful flowers and gentle slopes. There is also a trail here designed to accommodate wheelchair-bound people. Many of the trees on the left side of the highway are **Scouler Willows**, bushy low-lying trees which turn bright yellow in late October; they are found wherever there is moisture, but unlike other willows can also be found along the side of the highway where there is no obvious moisture. Scouler Willow is described more fully in Adventure 7.

8.3 (1.6) The road to the right just before the highway swings left at Mount Rose Summit leads to Mount Rose Campground. Park the car in the dirt area on the left side of the highway and walk back to the campground road. The trees on the left just before the campground road look like Lodgepole Pines, but just a little different. Most Lodgepole Pines have yellowish trunks, but these trees have weatherbeaten whitish trunks. The upper part of the trunks also have horizontal lines. They also have five needles in a bundle compared with Lodgepole Pine's two.

These are **Whitebark Pine** trees, and this is probably the only place you will see them in these Adventures. They are only found near treeline, in windy exposed places. The sketch on the next page shows some of the features of Whitebark Pine.

Both Lodgepole and Whitebark Pines are present in this area. Distinguishing the two trees from a distance is not easy (I drove along this stretch of highway many times before someone told me that these trees were here); but from close up you can easily distingush the two species by the number of needles.

What distinguishes Whitebark Pine from Western White Pine, the other five-needle pine in this area? Western White Pine has much smaller cones, and Whitebark Pine bark looks like Lodgepole Pine bark.

"popcorn" bark
is whitish

looks like Lodgepole Pine except:
- grows in clumps
- occurs above 8500 feet
- has five needles in a bundle
- commonly smaller with a gnarled trunk

Whitebark Pine

John Muir loved these trees!

top of tree generally
droops

1" needles radiate in groups,
sometimes are blue-green

Mountain Hemlock

Mount Rose Summit, at 8911 feet, is the highest pass over the Sierra Nevada open all year. It is also the highest elevation along a highway in the Lake Tahoe Basin, and is the only highway with Whitebark Pine along it. The top of Slide Mountain, on the right, is at 9694 feet; yet it is almost 1100 feet lower than the top of Mount Rose, the extinct volcano you can see about 2 1/2 miles north of here and the tallest mountain on the north side of the Lake Tahoe Basin. The weather observatory on top of Mount Rose was the first place with snow surveys, which are now used all over the world to predict seasonal water flow in snowy areas. The linear treeless areas on Slide Mountain are ski runs of Mount Rose Ski Area (a surprising name because the runs are on Slide Mountain).

The trees on the hill on the left of the highway a few hundred feet past the summit look a lot like Red Fir; but the leaders (tops) of these trees seem to be bent over. These are **Mountain Hemlock** (shown in the sketch on the previous page).

In *My First Summer in the Sierra*, John Muir described Mountain Hemlock as "the most beautiful conifer I have ever seen." For a tree lover like me, this a good day; I can see both Western White Pine and Mountain Hemlock.

Mountain Hemlock is most abundant on slopes like this — facing north and above 8000 feet. Mountain Hemlock apparently prefers northern slopes because it does not need much sunlight (it is shade-tolerant) and it needs to be in areas where deep snow lasts until relatively late in spring. The snow helps to keep the tree's roots from freezing, and the moisture it provides helps the tree. Other species growing at this altitude are much less shade-tolerant, so Mountain Hemlock dominates this stand.

Mountain Hemlock can survive the harsh climatic conditions herebecause it is flexible; when the wind blows, the tree bends instead of breaking (unlike Red Fir, whose brittle top is commonly snapped off during storms). In fact, Mountain Hemlock seedlings are so limber that they are sometimes bent over by snow, and as the snow is melting, suddenly spring up out of the snow.

9.3 (1.0) The solitary tree about 50 feet to the left of the highway on the hillside and 30 feet above the roadbed on the large curve to the right is an old Western White Pine. Pull off onto the dirt turnout on the right side of the highway and admire this tree; if you are even more ambitious (as I was), clamber carefully up the slope to check it out.

11.0 (1.7) (The entrance to Mount Rose Ski Area). Across the highway 0.2 mile further is a dirt road which heads almost back uphill. This road is the 20-minute-plus Side Trip B to examine **Washoe Pine** — if you take it, you will have to retrace your steps (but after reading this description you may consider it worthwhile). Side Trip B is found in Appendix H.

11.8 (0.8) The road to the right leads to the East Bowl of Mount Rose Ski Area (formerly Slide Mountain Ski Area). Most ski areas are located on the north and east sides of mountains, like this one, because the snow lasts longest in this quadrant: the eastern side of a mountain gets morning sun, and the temperature is lower in morning than afternoon; the sun is mostly in the southern half of the sky, so the northern side gets less sun (the very same conditions that favor Mountain Hemlock!).

    Across the highway are **Quaking Aspens** and Scouler Willows, sure signs that there is moisture in the soil.

12.4 (0.6) The rusted ski lift in the forest on the left side of the highway, abandoned before 1958, gives a good idea of how rapidly Quaking Aspens can grow here. This ski lift is in an old ski area now owned by the City of Reno, and used for schoolchildren to ski on winter weekends.

    As you round the curve to the left, pull off in the small turnout if there is space; otherwise proceed to the next one about 0.3 miles ahead, which has the sign "Slow Vehicle Turnout" before it. This is a great place for a vista of the Carson Valley and mountains beyond.

    If you are at the first turnout, you will be able to see all of Washoe Lake, a water supply for Washoe County which as a glacial lake was about twice its present size. The town behind it is New Washoe City. You can see the continuation of Nevada 431 below you; the buildings along it are about 400 feet lower. The highway twists and turns until it straightens out about 1400 feet below. The road you may be able to see on the mountainside ahead leads to Virginia City. The last large building you can see before the mountainside blocks your view is the Reno Hilton, which is actually about 300 feet below you.

This is the beginning of the "Basin and Range Province," which continues for hundreds of miles east of here and is characterized by mountains trending approximately north-south separated by desert valleys. Curiously, although the Lake Tahoe Basin rocks are similar to those in the Sierra Nevada Province, the geologic structure is similar to that in the Basin and Range Province.

The Carson Valley gets about 11 inches of precipitation a year, compared with the Lake Tahoe Basin with 20 inches plus. Jeffrey Pine (which has reappeared here at about 7400 feet) and the other common Lake Tahoe Basin species do not grow well with less than 20 inches of annual precipitation, so there are very few Tahoe tree species in the Carson Valley and the mountains beyond. Binoculars show that the conifers on those mountains are sparse and rounded rather than dense and conical like Tahoe conifers. Two species dominate; **Single-leaf Pinyon Pine** is the only North American pine with only one needle in a bundle; **Utah Juniper**, as the name implies, is found all the way from here to Utah. Because the increase of elevation in the mountains is sufficient to provide greater precipitation, lower temperatures and less evaporation than the Carson Valley, these two species can survive. Although there are few trees of these two species along the side of the highway on this Adventure, there are many Utah Junipers in Idlewild Park (Adventure 6). The large trees in the Carson Valley are "riparian" (riverbank) trees such as **willows** and **Fremont Cottonwood**.

18.2 (5.8) The first entrance to Galena Creek Park (operated by Washoe County) is to the left. This park has a well-signed nature trail, and you can get a free interpretative guide by asking at the ranger station. It takes about a half hour, and you won't see any trees not seen else-where in these Tree Adventures, but if you have the time it's a nice visit.

18.7 (0.5) Near the end of the Jeffrey Pine and White Fir trees, on both sides of the highway, is a stand of young Jeffrey Pine trees. These trees have about 10 to 15 horizontal branches; allowing for branches having fallen off, this means that they are about 20 years old, and the area was clear-cut about 20 years ago. On the hill to the left are logs remaining from the logging operation.

The slope from here to the bottom of the valley is the result of streams draining the glaciers on Mount Rose, creating what is known as an "outwash plain." There was so much material coming down the glacier, and the slope was so steep (eight degrees), that the streams never formed channels; instead, they formed fan-shaped deposits like this one. We will see other outwash deposits along the Truckee River near Verdi, and there I shall discuss glacial deposits.

25.1 (6.4) Just before you turn left onto U. S. 395 toward Reno, look at the curious structures a few hundred feet right of the highway. This is a geothermal power plant, constructed to take advantage of the hot rocks below capable of being used for electric power generation; the size of this plant testifies as to the amount of hot rock beneath you. Water is pumped into holes in the rock, which give off enough heat to turn the water to steam. This steam turns turbines to generate electricity.

On the right is Steamboat Creek, a stream which only flows above ground part of the year. The rest of the year a river flows underground to Lake Alexander, a small lake just south of Sparks. The Fremont Cottonwood trees on the right are getting their water from this underground river.

Why do the streams and rivers in this area go underground? The answer lies in the geology of this area. The mountains here were raised by geologic forces along faults on each side, and the valleys were lowered. These movements provided a low area to trap rocks and sand eroded from the mountains. Floods uncommon on a human time scale but common on a geologic time scale erode rock from the nearly vegetationless mountains and the nearly barren hillsides, washing it into the low area. So there is no rock in the middle of the valley, but instead thousands of feet of essentially sand. Water coming from the mountains has no solid riverbed, so it sinks as low into the "sand trap" as it can go. Even the Truckee River, which we are going to see in a few minutes, disappears into the desert at a place named Pyramid Lake.

The Comstock Lode silver and gold strike of 1858 in Virginia City created a demand for feed for the many animals involved in various aspects of the mining business, and alfalfa was raised to feed them. The old house surrounded by huge trees near the intersection of Nevada 431 and U.S. 395 marks the location of the first alfalfa farm in the Carson Valley. The huge Fremont Cottonwood trees surrounding the house were obviously planted to shade the house, which was built in 1864 (the year Nevada became a state). The biggest tree in the yard is in failing health, and by the time you read this may be gone. Still, it is the biggest Fremont Cottonwood I have seen in the area covered by these Adventures, and the other trees are pretty large too. The house is in the National Register of Historic Places, so history or architecture buffs may want to check it out; turn right on Zolezzi Road (at 26.3), then turn right on Old Virginia Street.

Wait a minute, you say. How could this tree be so big (8.1 feet in diameter) and yet be less than 150 years old? Well, tree size does not necessarily reflect age. Fremont Cottonwoods grow very quickly in diameter and height, given adequate moisture and the 3,500 plus hours annual sunshine the Reno area receives; but they also have a very short life expectancy. The table below illustrates this concept.

35.1 (10.0) U.S. 395 intersects Interstate 80 near downtown Reno here; take Interstate 80 West past downtown to the Keystone Exit (at 37.0).

In Adventure 6, you can explore Idlewild Park, one of Reno's three arboreta; this two-hour Adventure starts and ends at this exit.

Before you reach the city center, look to the left and right of the freeway. Many of the dark green conifers taller than houses are Giant Sequoia trees (see Adventure 6 for a description). They are very popular for yard and street planting in Reno because they grow very rapidly, given enough water. The Nevada Champion Giant Sequoia is in Reno; the table below compares this tree with Fremont Cottonwood and the slow-growing Single-leaf Pinyon Pine, two tree species native to the High Desert.

Tree	Age	Life Expectancy	Diameter	Height
This Fremont Cottonwood	150 years	150 years	8.1 feet	84 feet
Typical Single-leaf Pinyon Pine	150 years	300 years	1.0 feet	40 feet
Nevada Champion	45 years	2000 years+	5.0 feet	89 feet

If you would like to spend a little time and money at the casinos in Reno, please fill out the order blank at the back of this book instead and get some books for your relatives. You can't lose. But if it's April and you feel compelled to go downtown, go to the intersection of the Truckee River and Lake Street, two blocks east of Virginia Street, and check out the **Wisteria** which has taken over the second-floor railing.

0.0 (0.0) I'm starting the odometer at the Keystone Exit of Interstate 80 in case you went on Adventure 6.

1.6 (1.6) The bare mountain on the right under the transmission towers is Peavine Peak. Its elevation of 8266 feet is about the same as that of Granite and Verdi Peaks (the forested mountains straight ahead of you); but instead of being covered with tall conifers like them it has only sparse Singleleaf Pinyon Pine and Utah Juniper trees, and those are on its north and east sides. Where are the trees? By the time the moist Pacific air reaches here, it has been drained of most of its moisture, and so there is not enough to support a Sierra Nevada forest.

3.3 (1.7)   The rock outcrops to the right of the highway are tilted and twisted. This shows the power of the geologic forces that created both the Sierra Nevada and Basin and Range mountains.

7.0 (3.7)   As you cross the Truckee River after the Boomtown Exit, look straight ahead to see how fire has devastated a forest. In the summer of 1994, a forest fire burned the area in front of us, reaching within a couple hundred yards of the Gold Ranch Casino at the foot of the mountain ahead.

There are two other things to see from here. The first is the wooden boxy structure snaking along the side of the hill next to the river. This is a flume used to carry water to generate hydroelectric power. We will see these for the next 11 miles.

The second thing is the flat surfaces above the river bottom. As we travel west, notice these. There are several levels of these, although from here we can only see one level above the riverbank.

The lowest flat surface above streams is called a "floodplain." People love to build houses here: it is right next to the esthetically beautiful flowing stream; the ground is easy to build on because it has sand and gravel instead of rocks; it is flat and can be plowed easily; and it is only a few feet above a large supply of water for home use. But the term "floodplain" means just that: when the river can no longer hold all the water it is supplied, it overflows its banks and floods. When this happens, either the houses are swept away by raging torrents or they are damaged by the rocks, sand and mud carried in a flood. We have all seen television pictures of flooding on the Mississippi River floodplain.

Rivers and streams erode (remove) material in one place and deposit (add) it in another, always downslope and in response to gravity. They move the material within the rushing water. If water is traveling lazily, it transports sand and mud; if there is a great flood, it can transport cobbles and boulders. But when the flood subsides and water velocity and turbulence decrease, the larger sediment is dumped — in this case, on a floodplain. Sediments deposited here may have traveled all the way from the top of a Sierra Nevada mountain.

Glaciers also erode and deposit; in fact, they are much more efficient at erosion than rivers (ice is very abrasive, and rocks and sand and mud can ride on the ice). Glaciers are essentially rivers of ice, which move downhill when the ice reaches a thickness of about 150 feet; the Truckee River Canyon a few miles ahead of you was once filled with a glacier, which carried material on top of and inside the ice. However, glaciers have a place at which the ice melts faster than it flows downhill, called a "terminal moraine." There is no ice below this point, but water from the melting ice continues to flow downslope, though, and it dumps the material off this ice-and-rock dam, in a fan-shaped "outwash" deposit. The flat floodplains you will see for the next few miles are the remains of the outwash from Truckee River glaciers.

9.3   (2.3)   As you cross the Truckee near Verdi, note that there are multiple flat surfaces, one above the other. What happened here?

The picture of the flat floodplain and outwash plain is incomplete. During the time of glaciation the Sierra Nevada was rising, but in episodes instead of in continuous movement. A stream in equilibrium has a certain gradient (decrease of elevation with distance); but if the upstream end rises, the stream has to seek a new equilibrium. The result is that it cuts a new floodplain lower than the old one, and we can see several terraces. This is common in mountainous areas everywhere.

The outwash deposits on the local floodplains are from different periods of glaciation. For some reason, glaciers expand and contract over periods of thousand of years. Each expansion pulse provides a new set of deposits, although an untrained eye may not be able to distinguish them.

10.9 (1.6) As you ascend into the canyon, notice the yellow building and power lines across the river left of thehighway. This is one of four Sierra Pacific Power Company hydroelectric power plants on the Truckee River. Water has been diverted from the river a couple of miles upstream into the box-like wooden flume, and it flows in the flume to turbines here, which turn generators to generate electricity; after it has gone through the power plant, it goes back into the river (as you can see here). This is the same process used at Hoover Dam in Arizona and Nevada, but on a much smaller scale.

Hydroelectric power is quite feasible in this area because of the ready supply of river water and the steep slope of the river canyon. The vertical distance from the flume entrance to the turbine is called the "head." The amount of electricity generated depends on the head and the water flow rate. Double either the head or the flow rate and you double the electrical power output!

These power plants were built before the turn of the century to provide electricity to pump water out of the Comstock Lode mines; continuous pumping was necessary because otherwise the mines would fill with water and be useless. Today they are part of the power network for Reno.

The power generated in the four hydroelectric plants on this river supplies 8.7 megawatts of energy, enough for about 5600 homes.

17.3 (6.4) From the wide dirt turnout here you can see **Curl-leaf Mountain Mahogany**. This shrub is an integral part of the Mountain Chaparral on the east slope of the Sierra Nevada. Its thick green leaves make it look like

*1/2" canoe-shaped leaf
(looks like a succulent)*

*4" long curled,
hairy seedpod
(late summer)*

*small shrubs with
gnarled branches*

Curl-leaf Mountain Mahogany

a succulent plant. The leaves are well-suited for the climate where Chaparral grows — dry air, little pre-cipitation but much evaporation. Also seen here is **Bitterbrush** (described in Adventure 4).

18.2 (0.9)   After you cross the Truckee River and just before the Floriston Exit, you may want to pull out to the right onto a dirt area away from the Interstate, next to the two dams. (There is a sign saying "Emergency Parking Only," and is you are not bold you can take the Floriston Exit, then turn right onto a road traveling uphill. You can park there and get a vantage point for these dams, but you won't be as close)

One dam diverts some of the river water into the flume for a hydroelectric power plant downstream. The other is a low-water dam with a curious structure next to it. This is a fish ladder, constructed so fish can swim upstream
in early fall to spawn in streams where they were born. Some fish literally leap out of water in streams to surmount rocks in the streams, but they can only leap about four feet or so. High concrete dams would prevent them from spawning, and would eventually totally prevent reproduction. That's why the fish lad-ders were built.

20.7 (2.5) Around the gentle curve to right is a mountainside with bands of rounded rocks. This is not a good place to pull off, but there is one a few miles ahead where I will tell you the story of the volcanoes of this area.

    One of the main types of material here is a mixture of boulders, cobbles, gravels, sands and muds. Volcanic eruptions blew a mixture of rock, molten lava and gas into the earth's atmosphere. This material, so hot that it would incinerate you if you fell into it, soon rained onto the ground and mixed with the rounded river deposits already there. The whole mess then flowed downriver in a boiling flood. Eventually, the mess stopped, cooled and solidified, making the cemented rock typical of volcanic mudflows. You will be seeing this material all the way to Tahoe City, and you can distinguish it from glacial material by the fact that it looks like concrete.

21.7 (1.0) The highway suddenly emerges from the 1500-foot-deep canyon and suddenly there is a view of the Sierra Nevada Crest 20 miles distant.

23.5 (1.8) On the right, after the turn just before the Hirschdale Road Exit, is the site of a "small" forest fire. Forest fires are both terrible and wonderful to behold. They start when drought kills and dries trees to make them fuel for potential torches. A spark from a campfire or from lightning ignites this fuel. High winds fan the flames, making the fire hard to control. With prevailing winds from the west and southwest, forest fires here tend to burn eastward until they run out of fuel.

    This fire started in the campground across the highway, and quickly jumped the highway when the wind blew embers across the hundred-foot width of Interstate 80. It then went uphill to the right, fed by the burning of the Chaparral vegetation with high fuel content.

    This fire was contained before it could burn more than a few hundred acres, but two other fires (the one which ended at Verdi and one a few miles north of here) kept firefighters busy for weeks.

24.4 (0.9) The Hirschdale Road Exit leads to the flat-topped hill on the right. This is the dam for the Boca Reservoir, one of three reservoirs for water supply, recreation and flood control in this area. Boca Dam is 116 feet high and 1629 feet long. The total water storage of this reservoir is 40,901 acre-feet (less than 1/10 percent of the storage of Lake Tahoe). Boca Reservoir and two other reservoirs near here were built partly to supply irrigation water for Nevada farmers in drought years.

27.0 (2.6) The California Highway Patrol Weigh Station is the only good place to pull off the highway for a story about volcanoes, though it was not designed for geology field trips!

We are now in Martis Valley, a place where the terrain changes from hilly to flat, with mountains on all sides. The mountains on the right horizon mark the northern edge of the Truckee River Basin. Five miles away on the left is Mount Pluto, the site of Northstar Ski Area and part of the story of Lake Tahoe's origin.

Many of the mountains you can see from this spot are volcanic; Mount Pluto is one of two centers of volcanic eruption on the north edge of Lake Tahoe. As you drive from Truckee to Tahoe City, most of the rocks you will see are from volcanic flows.

Here is a scenario of what happened here from about three million years ago to about one million years ago. Most of the time things were very quiet, with rivers eroding the mountains around here. But in brief yet violent episodes, lava erupted onto the earth's surface.

Sometimes the lava came out in slow-moving flows. Like other fluids, the lava sought the lowest places, so the lava went down stream valleys until it reached places like this. Large-scale faulting had created a low, almost flat place, a good receptacle for the lava; the lava made the ancestral Martis Valley even flatter.

Sometimes the lava came out explosively, with Mt. St. Helens-like explosions ripping tops off mountains, and lava going down stream courses. In the process it mixed with stream rocks and water.

In places where the valley was narrow, the lava flow filled the valley and solidified, creating a dam behind it. Since volcanic rocks are relatively easy to erode, the stream water eventually broke through the dam. There is a stop at a place between Truckee and Tahoe City where this happened.

After volcanic activity ceased, glaciation took place in the Truckee River Canyon and the stream valley below Donner Pass, and the water from melting glaciers transported material toward Reno. Many of the flat surfaces in this valley are the tops of glacial outwash deposits.

30.0 (3.0 From this exit, California 267 heads 13 miles south over Brockway Summit (elevation 7199 feet) to Lake Tahoe's North Shore at Kings Beach. This is the first of four exits for the town of Truckee.

31.4 (1.4) On the left before the Central Truckee Exit, next to a dairy-barn-like building, is a round structure with 13 columns and two rocks inside it; the top rock is the Rocking Stone (see sidebar); to reach it, go under the freeway and turn left immediately onto High Street.

32.2 (0.8) At the U.S. 89 Exit to Lake Tahoe, you have a choice: you can exit here and head south toward Tahoe City 0.8 mile to the intersection of U.S. 89 and West River Road to Tahoe City (below), or you can continue on Interstate 80 on Side Trip C, where we shall explore glaciated terrain, the picturesque town of Truckee and the history of pioneers crossing the Sierra Nevada here. Side Trip C is found in Appendix B.

0.0 (0.0) (The odometer is reset to zero here) Turn left toward Tahoe City. This is the valley of the Truckee River, a meandering stream cut deeply into ridges of volcanic rocks on each side of the highway. The trees on the riverbank are Black Cottonwood and willows, on the mountainsides are mostly Jeffrey Pine and White Fir, but on the roadside are mostly Lodgepole Pines. Why? The answer lies in three characteristics of Lodgepole Pine.

First, Lodgepole Pine grows readily in disturbed areas, for example this one where there are many 20-year-old trees (check the horizontal branches on the trees). When the sides of the road were cleared of trees a few feet away from the pavement, the soil was disrupted. This made it more difficult for Jeffrey Pine to sprout, and the sun-loving, opportunistic Lodgepole Pine took over. Second, Lodgepole Pine prefers a wetter soil than Jeffrey Pine, and the water table is at river level, just a few feet below the road. Third, Lodgepole Pine is even less shade-tolerant than the intolerant Jeffrey Pine, so to thrive it must be at the side of a road.

Lodgepole Pine normally only reaches a height of about 100 feet, so many years from now the Jeffrey Pines will overtop the Lodgepole Pines and shade them out, killing them. But today you will see many more small Lodgepole Pines than Jeffrey Pines at roadside all the way to Tahoe City.

2.6 (2.6) On the left of the highway is a rock with bedding at a 40-degree angle. This rock not only shows how intense faulting was here, but it is also a great hiding place. In today's world with cars zipping by at 55 miles per hour, drivers are past it before they notice it. But in the last century, when stagecoaches passed this point at a few miles per hour, bandits could jump out from behind the rock to hold up the stage. This place was known as "Robber's Roost." At least one holdup did not go so well for the robbers, however; they were caught and hung.

5.4 (2.8) Pull off to the left at the entrance to Goose Creek Campground (there is no safe place on the right of the road near here), and I'll tell you a story of Fire and Ice.

Note how narrow the river valley is here. This is the site of some extraordinary events, although this place does not look unusual. By looking at the rock deposits around here, geologists have determined that this is the site of two huge dams which raised the level of Lake Tahoe to about the tops of the hills on each side of this valley.

****
The Rocking Stone and Other Truckee Oddities

The Rocking Stone is a seventeen-ton granite boulder atop an almost perfectly flat circular larger boulder 15 feet high, an odd arrangement possibly caused by a freak of Nature where glacier ice melted, settling the top rock exactly in the middle of the bottom rock, or by ancient peoples somehow placing the top rock on the bottom rock (take your pick). It is balanced such that it could be rocked with the touch of a finger (before someone stabilized it). John Muir visited this rock in the 1890s with prominent Truckee citizen C.F. Mc Glashan. Mc Glashan was apparently quite taken with these rocks, so he bought the land and built the odd gazebo-like structure you see as a museum. After glassing in the 14-sided structure, Mc Glashan built a house with the same architectural style next door (the house burned down in 1935, and was replaced by the odd-looking building, which was built as a gymnasium).

Into the odd museum he put both his butterfly collection and his extensive collection of Donner Party relics (he was the first person to write about the Donner Party, in 1879). His next oddity was a giant icicle: as preliminary engineering work for an ice skating palace, in 1894 he constructed a framework of light timbers and wire mesh, and added water to it every day. The water froze, making an icicle as tall as the gazebo. The experiment must have been successful; the next year he built a circular skating rink, with walls 50 feet tall and a giant toboggan slide. Water sprayed on the structure daily in winter created huge icicles. This tourist attraction put Truckee on the map as a winter destination, with visitors coming from as far away as San Francisco.

McGlashan also has one more claim to fame. He was part of the first party to survey the depth of Lake Tahoe, using fishing line and a bottle. In a traverse across the northern part of the Lake, the party managed to survey the exact deepest spot in the Lake at 1645 feet, a number that exactly matches with today's figure.

I would have liked to meet this man.

— Additional information in "Truckee" by Joanne Meschery

****

Both volcanic flows and glaciers flow downhill, and stream valleys are great places to flow downhill. About 1.9 million years ago, lava started pouring out of Mount Pluto and Mount Watson, two volcanoes a few miles east of here. With sporadic flows into the river valley near Tahoe City, the Truckee River could maintain its course at about its present elevation; but about 1.4 million years ago, the Big Chief Basalt (the flat-lying rock you see on the top of the canyon to the east) overwhelmed the river's capability to erode and made a lava dam 600 feet high here (raising the level of Lake Tahoe 600 feet). After a few thousand years, the Truckee River was able to cut down through these volcanic rocks, at this spot, and the Truckee River flowed at the present elevation again. Perhaps 1.3 million years ago, later flows near Tahoe City dammed the canyon upstream, this time to 800 feet above us. The Truckee River once again cut down to the present elevation.

About 1.2 million years ago, flows originating near Truckee forced the river course downstream to follow the edge of the flows, resulting in today's river course. (Much of the Truckee River's course was controlled by volcanic flows)

A few hundred feet ahead is Pole Creek, which today looks almost insignificant. But starting about 0.6 million years ago, a glacier present in Pole Creek's valley brought ice and rock into the narrow Truckee River Valley. Once again, it was a matter of supply of material versus the Truckee's ability to erode. About 0.5 million years ago, ice from the glacier crossed the narrow valley and made a glacial dam right here. Again the top of the dam (and Lake level) were 600 feet above us.

This time the dam was not cut down an inch at a time, but probably in one catastrophic event when the water leaked under the ice and the dam failed. Imagine a wall of water 600 feet high racing down this valley! This one event removed almost all of the dam, and today there is only scant evidence that this ever took place.

7.6 (2.2) Like Pole Creek, Squaw Creek was the site of a glacier. About 0.2 million years ago, glacial sediment made a 90-foot dam across the Truckee River. But this was only one glacial pulse; during most of the time of glaciation, the end of the glacier was apparently just upstream from here. When this happens, the terminal or end moraine stays in one place, a dam forms and impounds water behind it. Donner Lake is a good example of a lake formed by a glacial dam.

If post-glacial sedimentation fills glacial lakes the result is a flat valley floor with steeply-sloping sides, such as we see today in Squaw Valley and Yosemite Valley. It is a worthwhile few-minute drive to the head of the valley, where the flat floor meets a very steep mountainside. Squaw Valley has few trees on its floor because conditions are too moist to maintain a forest.

Squaw Valley also has a recreational area at its 8200-foot-elevation High Camp, which includes swimming, tennis and bungee jumping in the summer, and ice skating year-round. To reach it, you ascend in a gondola. If you are riding this gondola, be sure to look out the right side window on the trip up. There are some marvelous Mountain Hemlocks on the canyon to the north. And at the top, next to the tennis courts, there are some wonderful Western White Pines.

9.5 (1.9) Alpine Meadows is another glacial valley, but its floor is not as flat as Squaw Valley's, and apparently is not as wet (it is heavily forested).

11.0 (1.5) On the right side of the road are some rounded shrubs about ten feet tall. This is the only place in these Tree Adventures you are likely to see this important shrub, Blue Elderberry, which has beautiful umbrella-shaped flower clusters in spring and blue berries in late summer and fall. The berries are commonly used to make pies and wine. The sketch of Blue Elderberry on the next page will help you identify it.

umbrella-shaped flower
clusters, 2"-8"

1/4" round,
blue-gray fruit

finely-toothed compound leaves
with 5 to 9 leaflets -- 5"-8"

Blue Elderberry

12.8 (1.8) The quarry on the left of the highway shows some of the rocks deposited in this area. The bottom rocks are from volcanic flows about two million years ago; the top rocks are from later river sedimentation. The inclination of 10 to 16 degrees demonstrates that there has been a lot of tilting in this part of the Truckee River Basin.

Around the bend to the left is Tahoe City; the last street before the end of this Adventure at the "Y" is Fairway Drive, which leads to the only entry along our Adventures to the Tahoe Rim Trail (see the sidebar on the next page). This Adventure ends at 13.3.

****

Volunteer Trails

These days, with Government money for building and maintaining hiking trails hard to come by, it's not surprising that people wanting trails through beautiful country like the Sierra Nevada resort to volunteerism. There are three cases in point in these Adventures. The Pacific Crest Trail stretches 2,200 miles from the Washington-British Columbia border to Southern California. This trail was conceived in 1926, and in the 1930s much of the trail was constructed with the help of monetary grants and volunteer labor in Washington and Oregon. But the California segment, much of it connecting mountain crests through very rough country, was not started until around 1972. A large portion of the Southern California segment was through private property, and since access was never granted for trail construction, this segment still has to go along highways. The PCT traverses the western boundary of the Truckee River Basin from north of Donner Pass to Echo Summit, crossing Interstate 80 near Donner Summit.

The Tahoe Rim Trail was a spinoff from the PCT and uses part of it. This trail, circling the Lake Tahoe Basin, was conceived in 1981, and construction started in 1984. By ten years later, about 83 of the planned 107 miles not on the PCT had been completed; parts not completed include the segments south of California 89 near Tahoe City and north and south of Mount Rose Highway near Mount Rose Summit.

Some of the money raised for the Tahoe Rim Trail was earmarked for the 7000-foot Whole Access Trail at Tahoe Meadows. This trail has a smooth and solid surface so that wheelchair-bound people and others can enjoy the wonders of Tahoe.

****

ADVENTURE 6

Idlewild Park

This Adventure starts at the Keystone Exit of Interstate 80 one mile west of downtown Reno. Head under the freeway (south). After a couple of traffic lights and just before the bridge heading uphill, take the street just to the right of the bridge. Where this dead-ends, turn right for one block and cross the bridge on your left. Immediately after this bridge turn right onto Idlewild Drive. A hundred yards or so farther is a lake with seemingly milllions of ducks and Canada Geese. This is Idlewild Park. Turn right at the sign advertising this park as the official arboretum for the City of Reno, and park either along the side of this road or the first road to the right (Mastrioanni Drive).

Before you get out of your vehicle, let me tell you a little bit about this city and this park. Reno is one of those special cities designated as "Tree City U. S. A."; in fact, it was the first city in Nevada so designated, in 1982. This is very interesting for a city with too little natural precipitation to grow many trees. So why do so many different trees grow here? Reno's climate is not too hot, not too cold, and (with irrigation) there is enough water.

Idlewild Park contains 49 acres. It was bought by the City of Reno in 1921 for $23,500.00 to be used as a free campground for tourists one mile out of town; instead, it was made into a city park, complete with a fish hatchery, a zoo and swimming pool, and was named in a city-wide contest. In 1927 it was the site of the Lincoln Highway Exposition, built to commemorate the first transcontinental highway (now known as U.S. 40, which parallels Interstate 80). The California Building, which you will pass on your tour, was built by California for the exposition to honor the dead from the First World War.

Idlewild Park is unusual in two ways. First, there are many non-native species here because for decades people in charge of recommending and planting trees in public areas of Reno had an interest in trying to grow trees from other parts of the country and the world; second, at least three Nevada Champion trees are present in this park.

Although the park has more than 100 species of trees and shrubs, the accompanying guide will only list the 43 most interesting and enlightening.

During our tour you will not only see a huge variety of trees and shrubs, but also will be learn about the suitability of various trees for yard, street and park planting (a tree suitable for one type of environment may not be suitable for another).

I'm supplying maps and sketches of each tree to guide you in case my verbal descriptions do not suffice; tree numbers in the text refer to the maps.

As you wander around looking at the trees in this park, please take caution: the ducks and geese here only do three things well. The first is waddling; the second is eating; and the third is the result of their eating. Please be careful where you step!

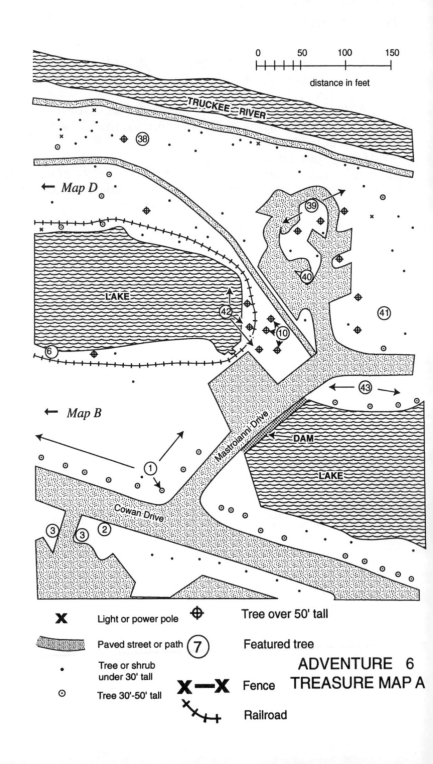

0   50   100   150
distance in feet

TRUCKEE RIVER

38

← Map D

39

40

41

LAKE

42

6

10

← Map B

43

DAM

Mastroianni Drive

1

LAKE

Cowan Drive

3   3   2

X   Light or power pole   ⊕   Tree over 50' tall

▨▨   Paved street or path   ⑦   Featured tree

•   Tree or shrub
under 30' tall
                                ADVENTURE   6
⊙   Tree 30'-50' tall   X—X   Fence   TREASURE MAP A

✕✛   Railroad

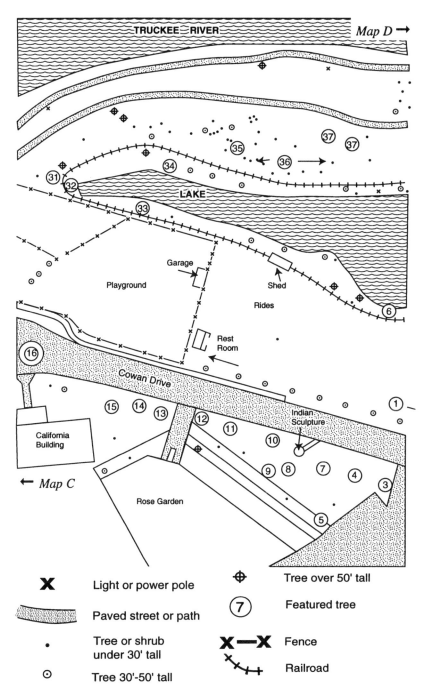

TRUCKEE RIVER   *Map D* →

LAKE

Garage

Shed

Playground

Rides

⑥

Rest Room

⑯

Cowan Drive

California Building

← *Map C*

Rose Garden

Indian Sculpture

① ⑮ ⑭ ⑬ ⑫ ⑪ ⑩ ⑨ ⑧ ⑦ ④ ③ ⑤

㉛ ㉜ ㉝ ㉞ ㉟ ㊱ ㊲ ㊲

X   Light or power pole

          Paved street or path

•   Tree or shrub under 30' tall

⊙   Tree 30'-50' tall

⊕   Tree over 50' tall

⑦   Featured tree

X—X   Fence

╈╈   Railroad

ADVENTURE 6   TREASURE MAP B

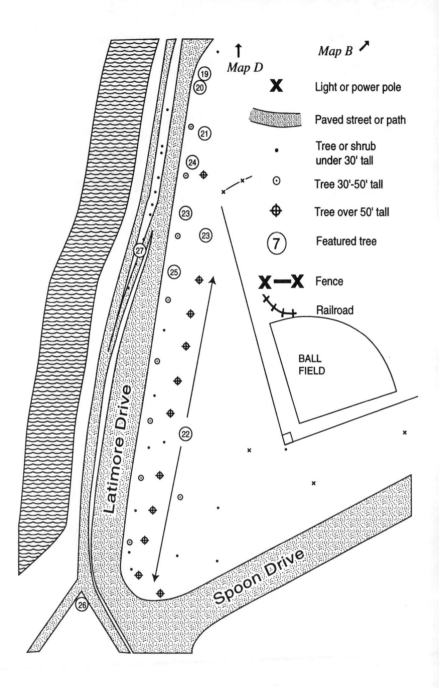

Map B ↗

↑
Map D

X   Light or power pole

   Paved street or path

 • Tree or shrub under 30' tall

 ⊙ Tree 30'-50' tall

 ⊕ Tree over 50' tall

 ⑦ Featured tree

X—X   Fence

   Railroad

BALL FIELD

Latimore Drive

Spoon Drive

ADVENTURE 6
TREASURE MAP C

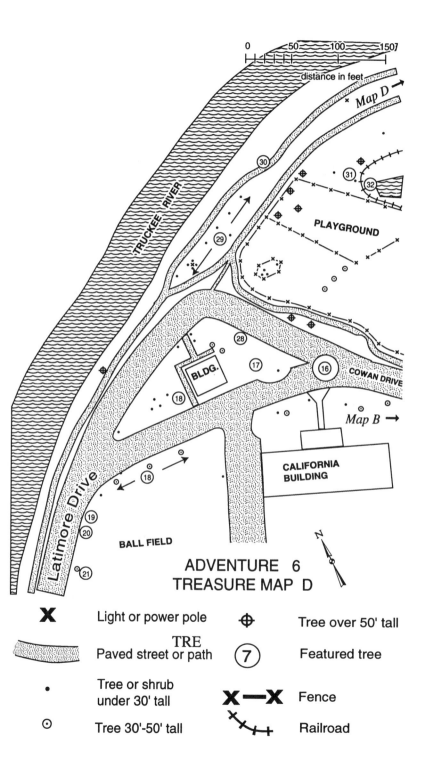

distance in feet

Map D →

TRUCKEE RIVER

(30)

(29)

(31)
(32)

PLAYGROUND

(28)

BLDG.

(17)

(16)

COWAN DRIVE

(18)

Map B →

CALIFORNIA
BUILDING

(18)

Latimore Drive

(19)

(20)

BALL FIELD

(21)

N

ADVENTURE 6
TREASURE MAP D

X   Light or power pole   ⊕   Tree over 50' tall

          TRE
Paved street or path   (7)   Featured tree

•   Tree or shrub
          under 30' tall   X—X   Fence

⊙   Tree 30'-50' tall   ⊬⊬⊬   Railroad

12" compound leaves

4"-6"
leaflets

3"
seedpod

seedpods turn brown,
stay on tree all winter

Green Ash

leaf widest near tip
with 5 to 7 lobes

flower spikes
1' long

1"-2" spiny fruit has
brown chestnut inside

Common Horsechestnut

Callery Pear (another
species at Idlewild) has
tiny or no fruits but is
covered with blossoms
in spring

2"-5"
fruit

glossy 2"-3" leaf
is finely toothed

yellow, orange or red fall colors

Fruiting Pear

This Adventure starts at the dam on Mastroianni Drive. From here, head toward the road you turned off to get to the dam. On your right is a row of three **Green Ash** trees (Tree 1) which continues down Cowan Drive to the right. This State Tree of South Dakota is the most-often planted street tree in the west and a it has a nice yellow color in autumn. This is one of the reasons for planting trees in parks — to give color; I'll tell you more about this as the tour progresses. In fall the branches are loaded with "samaras" (seedpods)). Unlike Maple samaras, Ash samaras contain single seeds. The objective is the same, however: the seeds twirl downward when they leave the tree, and wind carries them a distance away from the tree.

If you ever go rowing or kayaking, chances are that your oars are made of Green Ash.

The next part of the tour will feature trees on Cowan Drive. After you cross the street, turn right. The young tree with the large palmate (hand-shaped) leaves is a **Common Horsechestnut** (Tree 2); it was also planted to provide color, in this case flower color. This tree has pinkish white flower spikes almost a foot long. Some varieties drop numerous spiny nuts on sidewalks, so this is not a good tree for city streets.

Flanking the parking lot driveway ahead are two **Fruiting Pears** (Tree 3). They are covered with white blossoms in early spring; the glossy, healthy dark green leaves turn orange to red in fall. The fruits are edible, but they make a mess on the sidewalk. For this reason pears, as well as other fruit trees, are prohibited from being planted along Reno streets.

Pears were originally imported from China, but are planted all over the United States today.

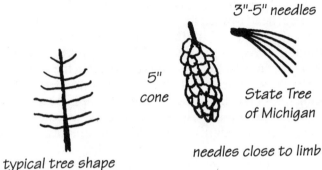

3"-5" needles

5" cone

State Tree of Michigan

typical tree shape

needles close to limb

Eastern White Pine

mature trees are flat-topped
with horizontal branches

branches are
pointed at end

2"-3" cone

green cones turn
brown in fall
(upright on branch)

radiating 1" needles are silvery gray

Atlas Cedar

mature trees are flat-topped
with horizontal branches

radiating 1"
needles are
bright green

cones are like Atlas
Cedar but a little
larger

Cedar of Lebanon

The next tree, an **Eastern White Pine** (Tree 4 on Map 2), is a native of the eastern United States, where it is valued for timber and Christmas trees. The needles provide a refreshing green color in this park setting.

The silvery green yet exotic conifer tree about 50 feet behind the Eastern White Pine may look familar to you (it is a common ornamental tree in the West) but it is not even a native of the United States: it hails from the Atlas Mountains of North Africa. This tree is an **Atlas Cedar** (Tree 5), one of three Cedar species. At maturity, this tree will be flat-topped and even more picturesque.

Look behind you; next to the lake is another exotic-looking tree with a flat top. This is the other species of Cedar found here in the park; it is a **Cedar of Lebanon** (Tree 6). A native of the Middle East, this tree is on the flag of Lebanon; but because of centuries of tree cutting and decades of war there, you probably have a better chance of seeing a majestic tree such as this in the United States. In my opinion, this is the most wonderful tree in this park.

Wait a minute; we've looked at six trees so far, and none of them is a native of this region So why are they in Idlewild Park? The answer is in two parts: first, many of them are readily available in nurseries in the Reno area; second, the people responsible for planning and planting trees in this park for many years (now referred to as "Urban Foresters") have decided to provide park-enjoyers with some great-looking trees.

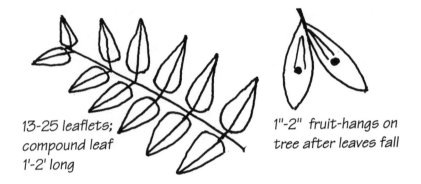

13-25 leaflets;
compound leaf
1'-2' long

1"-2" fruit-hangs on
tree after leaves fall

Tree of Heaven

native to China -
discovered 1948 -
popular here now

needles

foliage turns
brown in fall,
then falls off

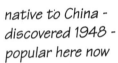

1/2" cone

looks like Coast Redwood
but trees are wider, shorter

Dawn Redwood

leaves glossy, dark green -
turn red in fall

2"-5"
leaves

1/2" dark
blue
fruit
in Idlewild, still a small tree

Black Tupelo

The next tree is non-native too. Between you and the wooden sculpture of an Indian is a **Tree of Heaven** (Tree 7), a native of China. Introduced to the United States in 1784, this tree typifies almost all of the reasons why an Urban Forester would want to plant a park tree. First, the female tree has beautiful red flowers in Spring. Second, in winter the seedpods hang on to the tree and provide more than bare branches for you to see. Third, Tree of Heaven is one of the few trees which thrives in cities. It seems that nothing can kill these trees; in fact, this may be the only bad thing about these trees; spreading by root suckers, they can take over areas if not controlled.

This particular tree is the Nevada Champion Tree of Heaven.

The three non-native trees directly behind the wooden sculpture may be the most remarkable trees in the park. **Dawn Redwood** (Tree 8), from central China, was first identified from fossil remains; it was not found in nature until the mid-1940s. Since then it has become a popular yard, street and park tree.

This tree is remarkable in another respect. Almost all conifers keep at least some of their leaves all winter, and these trees are commonly referred to as "evergreens." This tree is an exception; all its needles turn brown and fall off each winter.

Between the Dawn Redwoods and the walkway is a young **Black Tupelo** (Tree 9), a native of the eastern United States (I've never been to Tupelo, Mississippi, but I can guess what tree is very common there). This tree was chosen because its shiny green leathery oval leaves turn blazing orange to scarlet in fall.

Although this tree is not commonly planted in Reno, it shows some promise as a yard and street tree; so consider this planting as a local experiment.

young trees have
Christmas tree shape

cones open fall

3"-4"

end view of twig -
sharp stiff 1"
needles on all sides

State Tree of Colorado and Utah

Colorado Blue Spruce

bluish gray needles and twigs

branching pattern

twigs have diamond pattern

Sierra Juniper

leaves turn brilliant orange to red in fall

star-shaped leaf
has toothed edges

5"-7"

fruit is spiny 1" ball

Sweetgum

Some trees are beautiful all year because of the color of their leaves. The **Colorado Blue Spruce** (Tree 10) next to the sculpture is one of these. A favorite yard tree also because it looks like a young symmetrical Christmas tree, this tree is the State Tree of Colorado.

The branches go all the way to the ground, a typical situation for conifers. Sure, this tree is great in a yard or in a park, but this tree would block visibility for automobiles; for this reason neither this nor any other conifer is not allowed as street trees in Reno.

Finally, a native tree! The 50-foot-tall conifer past the Colorado Blue Spruce is a **Sierra Juniper** (Tree 11), probably about 50 years old. This tree rarely looks this good where it grows on the bare granite slopes of the Sierra Nevada (for example, the monarch at the entrance to Vikingsholm in Adventure 7). From about 7000 feet to tree line, these trees endure anything Nature can dish out and assume gnarled shapes. The oldest trees in the Lake Tahoe area are Sierra Junipers, with estimated ages up to about 2000 years.

Next to the walkway to the Rose Garden is another tree selected for its blazing fall colors, **Sweetgum** (Tree 12). The leaves make you think it is a maple; but it actually is of the genus Liquidambar (what a great name). The "corky wings" on its smaller twigs make it interesting in the winter when there are no leaves (another reason why Urban Foresters would want such a tree in a park).

In the eastern United States, this tree is used for making furniture, veneer, interior trim and knick-knacks, because it has a beautiful grain.

The numerous spiny balls which fall from the tree in fall and winter make it undesirable for street planting; they either make a mess to clean off sidewalks or are hazardous for pedestrians. Also, this species is riparian and will not grow well on dry sites.

typical leaf
2"

yellow to red
fall color

orange to red
1/4" berries
in clusters

some species may have thorns!

Hawthorns

leaves up to 1 foot long!

2"
flowers in
5"-6" panicles

fruits 12"-18" long -
hang on all winter

Northern Catalpa

fall color yellow

a "fossil tree"

female trees have
smelly, messy 1" fruits

fan-shaped leaf 1" to 2"

Ginkgo

The small tree on the other side of the walkway is a **Hawthorn** (Tree 13). Botanists go nuts trying to differentiate species in Hawthorns (there are over 100 species native of North America), so we'll just think of this as a generic Hawthorn. Hawthorns, as you might guess from the name, generally contain thorns, which make them undesirable near children (consequently, they are not allowed as street trees in Reno); however, hawthorns are so popular for urban planting that there are many varieties, some of which have few or no thorns.

Hawthorns typically have red berries, which ripen in fall and provide winter colors after the leaves fall (yet another reason for planting them in a park setting).These berries are also enjoyed by birds, so Hawthorn is a good tree if you like to watch birds.

The next tree near the street is a visual treat at any time of the year. In spring heart-shaped leaves grow to almost a foot in size; in late spring and early summmer upright pyramidal clusters of trumpet-shaped white flowers delight the eye; in fall and winter long bean-like seedpods droop from the bare branches. **Northern Catalpa** (Tree14) is native to the midwestern United States.

The next tree will have an awkward shape throughout its youth; but the species is not young. The **Ginkgo** (Tree 15), a native of eastern China, has been growing on Earth for 150 million years. As might be expected from such a long-lived species, this tree is pretty tough. It is a common urban tree, because it is nearly impervious to pests and diseases. It is often planted because of its unusual fan-shaped leaves, which turn bright yellow in the fall.

Care has to be taken in planting these trees, however, The female trees bear round one-inch fruits which are not only messy but also emit a disagreeable odor. For this reason only male trees are planted.

Ginkgo is botanically interesting because it is more closely related to conifers than to other broadleaved trees and because it is the only surviving member of its family.

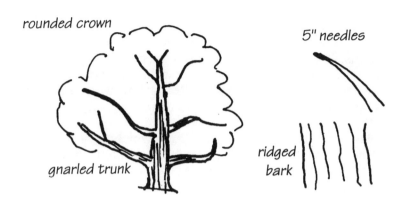

rounded crown

gnarled trunk

5" needles

ridged bark

Bishop Pine

leaves turn brown, stay on tree all winter

1/2" acorn

typically five lobes, leaves are pointed

Pin Oak

7"-8" compound leaf

7"-18" twisted seedpod stays on treeall winter

bark has long scaly ridges

many varieties have thorns on trunk or branches

Honeylocust

The gnarled large conifer in the traffic circle is the Nevada Champion **Bishop Pine** (Tree 16), which is a native of the California coast. Loggers of the nineteenth century passed over this tree in favor of the Coast Redwoods, which didn't have coarse-grained, knotty, pitchy wood like this tree. In the windy, harsh conditions along the coast, these trees grow gnarled and misshapen; in gentler climates they have a beautiful umbrella shape.

Bishop Pine cones do not fall off the tree like cones of most other pines. They may remain on the tree for years, and the tree bark may grow around them.

Between the Bishop Pine and the small building is a **Pin Oak** (Tree 17 on Map 3). A native of the midwestern United States, this is a favorite street tree because of its graceful crown symmetry. The lower branches point downward, so this tree has to be pruned to provide for safety for pedestrians.

The fast-growing tree has scarlet foliage in fall; the leaves turn brown but hang onto the tree all winter, providing winter interest.

This is another riparian tree; it will not grow well on dry sites or where pH exceeds 7.0.

The four trees on the left side of the street are **Honeylocust** (Tree 18), another tree which is interesting year-round. Although the first leaves of many broadleaved trees are lighter in color than later leaves (because they don't have as much chlorophyll), the first leaves appreaing on some varieties of Honeylocust are yellow, a striking color indeed. Later the leaves turn the normal green, and yellow flower spikes make the tree beautiful once again. In fall the leaves turn yellow. After the leaves fall, black twisted seedpods several inches long hang from bare branches.

Originally Honeylocust trees had an undesirable feature: sharp pointed thorns sticking out from the trunk and branches made them unsafe for pedestrians, especially young children. Because this tree had so many strong points, however, thornless varieties were developed, of which these trees are good examples.

Honeylocust may have different forms: the large tree next to the small building across the street is also a Honeylocust. Not only is this tree differently-shaped than the ones behind you, but it also has few seedpods; this is an example of the variety of individual trees in the same species.

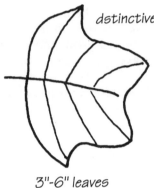

dstinctive leaf shape

flowers green-yellow-orange
(look like tulips)

yellow autumn leaf color

3"-6" leaves

Tulip Tree

reddish bark with horizontal lines

1/2" beautiful white,
pink or red flowers

1"-3" leaves skinny, fine-toothed

Cherry

largest of Western oak trees;
member of White Oak Group

2"-4"
leaves

1"-2" acorn

Valley Oak

ght. The first tree you encounter is a **Tulip Tree** (Tree 19). Not only does it have uniquely-shaped leaves, but it also has greenish-yellowish-orangeish flowers shaped like tulip flowers in summer. In fall, the leaves turn yellow.

A native of the eastern United States, the Tulip Tree is an important timber tree there, sometimes growing to heights of 150 feet. The light-colored wood is in great demand for cabinets under the trade name of "whitewood." This tree is the official state tree of Tennessee and Indiana.

The three-trunked tree next to the Tulip Tree is a **Cherry** (Tree 20). Note that the bark a few feet above the ground is fairly smooth and sort of cherry-colored. Most fruit trees have bark with this appearance. There are many varieties of cherries, both providing fruits and just flowering (like the Japanese Cherries for which Washington, D.C. is famous). Cherries are only one group of a genus that also includes peaches, plums, apricots and almonds.

Fifty feet down the street and 25 feet left of it is a small tree. This young **Valley Oak** (Tree 21) is a native of the Central Valley of California. Give this tree 100 or 150 years; it may become the most magnificent tree in the park. Valley Oak is considered the monarch of the oaks of the western United States. The National Champion Valley Oak, in California, is the largest oak tree in the United States.

Valley Oak shows great promise in this setting because it tolerates drought well and grows very rapidly (another desirable characteristic for urban and park trees).

The round plaque in the ground next to this tree was donated. The City of Reno is encouraging citizens to sponsor such plaques; they would love to talk with you.

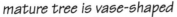

mature tree is vase-shaped

3" leaf is highly toothed

many branches dead or broken

State Tree of North Dakota, Nebraska and Massachusetts

diamond-shaped bark

American Elm

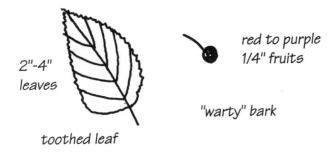

2"-4" leaves

red to purple 1/4" fruits

"warty" bark

toothed leaf

Hackberry

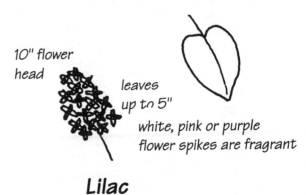

10" flower head

leaves up to 5"

white, pink or purple flower spikes are fragrant

Lilac

The large trees about 40 feet left of this street are **American Elms** (Tree 22 on Map 4), a native of the eastern and central United States and the state tree of Massachusetts and Nebraska. American Elm has historically been one of the most popular street and park trees, possibly because of the graceful vase-shaped crown of mature trees. These trees, obviously much older than the Park, may have been planted along an early road. Walk toward the first tree. You may see two shallow round depressions along the tree line before this tree. What are these? These are where two elm stumps were removed. You see, American Elm tends to die. In 1930 Dutch Elm Disease was inadvertently introduced into the United States; since then it has killed many beautiful American Elm trees. Elms are illegal to plant anywhere in Reno — including private property — because they are prolific seed producers, but the brittle branches falling also create hazards.

Near one of the depressions is a young tree. If American Elm represents the past for Idlewild Park, **Hackberry** (Tree 23) represents the future. In the description of the dam at Tahoe City, I mentioned WATER. With an annual precipitation of only eight inches and a rapidly growing population, it makes sense that in the future watering of trees in Reno is going to be either drastically curtailed or prohibited. So what is needed is trees like Hackberry that can be grown with little water. Two other positive features of Hackberry: unlike American Elm, it is relatively pest-free in the Intermountain West; and it does not produce millions of unwanted, messy seeds.

The three species of Hackerry in Idlewild Park are Common Hackberry, Western Hackberry and Chinese Hackberry.

The three shrubs on the side of the road about 40 feet from the Valley Oak are **Lilac** (Tree 24). Lilac, a native of the Old World, is a popular shrub because of its beautiful and fragrant spikes of flowers in spring.

fall color yellow-brown

twigs have "corky wings"

1" acorn

6"-12" leaves
are among
largest of oaks

White Oak Group

Bur Oak

"un-maple-like" leaves

yellow flowers

typical maple
samara (seedpod)

2"-3"
leaves

yellow, orange and
red fall color

Amur Maple

flower cluster stalks
look like smoke

purple leaves turn
gold, orange and
red in fall

late summer -
striking smoky
appearance

Purple-leaf Smokebush

The small tree next to the street between the last two pine trees is **Bur Oak** (Tree 25), which may be a valuable tree for Reno in the future when drought-resistant trees are desired. This tree is a good urban tree because it can withstand heat, drought, cold and a range of soil types. Its leaves are among the largest in the Oak genus (up to 12 inches long); they turn brown in fall and stay on the trees all winter. Twigs frequently have corky "wings."

Where the street curves to the left, just past where the bike path splits there is an **Amur Maple** (Tree 26). This tree's leaves do not look like that of a maple, but the fall colors are definitely maple-like: the leaves turn yellow, orange, red or purple.

Turn around and walk back on the bike path. Along the way there are many shrubs and small trees. About 40 feet past the small tree is the shrub **Purple Leaf Smoketree** (Tree 27), so named because when the flowers dry up the flower clusters look like puffs of smoke. These shrubs can tolerate high desert conditions such as are found in Reno.

new spring foliage is
salmon red!

compound leaf has 7-15 leaflets

3"
leaves
are deeply lobed

2" seedpods look like Chinese
lanterns, hang on all winter

Goldenrain Tree

toothed leaves are
commonly lobed
(distinctive)

the tree of the silkworm in China

White Mulberry

Feature	Fremont Cottonwood	Black Cottonwood
leaves	triangular, as wide as long coarsely toothed	longer than wide finely toothed
mature bark	diamond pattern	vertical furrows

Fremont vs. Black Cottonwood

About 30 feet past the small building, near the street leading to the Bishop Pine, is a **Goldenrain Tree** (Tree 28 on Map 5), a native of eastern Asia but quite popular in the United States. Though this tree has no autumn color, the new spring foliage is salmon red, turning blue-green later. The large golden-yellow flowers of early summer ripen as copious hanging clusters of seedpods looking like small paper lanterns. These seedpods remain when the leaves fall, providing winter interest.

Past where the bike path splits are five young trees of the same species, **White Mulberry** (Tree 29). Like Hackberry, White Mulberry does well in Reno because it is a fast-growing shade tree which will grow well in an area with hot, dry summers. The foliage of Mulberry is eaten by silkworms, which then produce silk. Silk production was attempted in California, but it was unsuccessful.

Mulberry fruits are often eaten by birds before people can pick them; if people pick the tasty fruits, their hands and clothes are stained. If neither birds nor people harvest the fruits, they make a mess on the sidewalk. For these reasons, fruitless varieties of White Mulberry have become popular; the trees here are of a fruitless variety.

Notice that the trees become smaller as you walk east. Why is this? I don't know, but my best guess is that the trees on the west shade out the ones on the east (you are walking east).

The huge tree that the bike path goes around is a **Fremont Cottonwood** (Tree 30), a member of the same genus as Black Cottonwood. Fremont Cottonwood is native to this area. In fact, it was first found in 1844, in this county, near Pyramid Lake (Pyramid Lake has another claim to fame: it is where the Truckee River — to your left — disappears underground).

All cottonwoods like to grow near running water, and there are many along the margin of the river. But they are also found in the park a few hundred feet from the river. How can this be?

The ground beneath you is made of old riverbed sediments, and is partly sand. If you were to dig twenty feet or so, the ditch would fill with water because water travels through the sand so well.

By the way, the bike path is on the levee of the river. This particular one is probably man-made, but levees are quite natural. They result when the river floods. Flooding rivers carry lots of sand because the water is turbulent enough to suspend the sand.

*leaves silvery gray underneath;
distinctive leaf shape*

bark has scaly ridges

*5"-7"
leaves*

Silver Maple

distinctive leaf shape

*2"-4"
leaves*

*leaves turn bright reds
and oranges in fall*

Trident Maple

*toothed edge,
straight veins*

*3/4" "cones"
in winter*

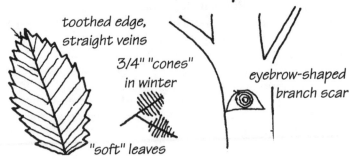

*eyebrow-shaped
branch scar*

"soft" leaves

White Alder

When the river overflows its banks, the water slows down and can no longer support the sand, and the sand is dumped. This happens over countless storms and a levee such as this is built up.

As you walk down the levee toward the creek, look at the two large trees twenty feet apart. One is another Fremont Cottonwood, but the other is a **Silver Maple** (Tree 31). A native of eastern and central North America, Silver Maple was planted as a street tree for many years because of its size and beautiful shape. Also, the leaves have interest: the wind turns over the leaves to show a silvery white underside. In fall the leaves turn yellow.

There are three reasons for the decline in this tree's popularity in urban settings. First, it has shallow roots which tend to break up sidewalks. Second, it is a water-loving tree, and it tends to destroy water mains in its search for water. Third, the branches and limbs are brittle, and break off during storms, creating a hazard and a mess. For these reasons maples are not good choices as street trees in Reno.

Twenty feet ahead, between the railroad track and the creek, is a Sierra Nevada native, **White Alder** (Tree 32). This is another water-loving tree — the pioneers traveling west in the nineteenth century looked for groves of alder trees because that meant permanent streams, and thus water for people and livestock.

White Alder is unusual because, although it is not a conifer, it has cones. These stay on the tree all winter, providing winter interest. Believe it or not, Alder cones are gold-plated and sold as miniature "pine cones" in gift shops! (This is probably better than wearing a 7-inch Jeffrey Pine cone as an earring)

White Alder is useful to other plants because it is a nitrogen fixer: bacteria living symbiotically on White Alder roots convert free nitrogen into nitrates which can be used as a natural fertilizer.

Trident Maple (Tree 33 on Map 6) is the tree ahead of you on the right between the creek and the fence. A native of eastern Asia, this tree is frequently planted as a street tree in Japan, partly because it can withstand urban stresses. This tree is interesting to us because it has an ususual-shaped leaf, and because its foliage is blazing in fall.

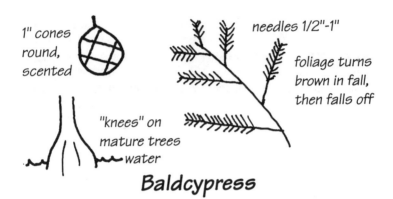

1" cones round, scented

needles 1/2"-1"

foliage turns brown in fall, then falls off

"knees" on mature trees — water

Baldcypress

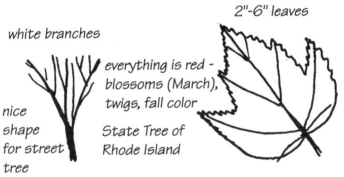

2"-6" leaves

white branches

everything is red - blossoms (March), twigs, fall color

State Tree of Rhode Island

nice shape for street tree

Red Maple

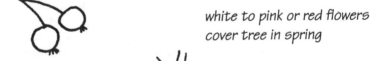

white to pink or red flowers cover tree in spring

compact form - usually small tree

fruit - less than 2" (if larger, tree is apple)

Crabapple

Walk along the tracks about 100 feet, looking toward the creek. You will spot an inconspicuous tree with tiny leaves along the creek bank. This relative of the Dawn Redwood also drops its leaves each fall. It is **Baldcypress** (Tree 34).

Remember all those adventure movies you saw where the people were rowing a boat through the evil-looking swamp? There were trees with slimy moss hanging down, and which were wider just above water line. These were Baldcypress, a tree which thrives in standing water. The tree widens a lot toward the base to help support it. The wide bases, called"cypress knees", have an interesting wood grain and are sawn into slices to be used for tables and clocks; the wood is very resistant and is used for dock and pier pilings.

Continue down the tracks. Across them about 100 feet ahead is a tree with dark bark on the trunk and white bark on the branches and limbs. This tree is **Red Maple** (Tree 35). It is a native of the eastern United States.

Red Maple is aptly named: during winter the buds are large and red, and burst forth into red blossoms in March. When the flowers are pollinated, they develop into reddish samaras; and the leaves turn red in autumn. There are many Red Maples in this part of the park. See if you can spot some more as you walk.

Red Maple shares some undesirable features with Silver Maple: its requires lots of water and it tends to be weak-wooded, shallow-rooted and prone to decay.

Just past the Red Maple are five small trees alongside the railroad track. These are a type of apple, known as **Crabapples** (Tree 36). The distinction between apples and crabapples is the size of the fruits, 2 inches in diameter or more for apples.

Although crabapples are edible, the tree is usually grown for its flowers. The fruiting varieties have bursts of pinkish white to red blossoms which appear before the tree leafs out, and the yellow, orange or red fruits sometimes hang on after the leaves fall. Most non-fruiting varieties have no fall color but have even more profuse gorgeous blossoms. Fruiting varieties may have good color, but are prohibited as street trees in Reno because of the mess the fruits make.

needles are barbs, pointing away from bark

cones are egg-sized

mature bark is cinnamon-colored, spongy, with deep furrows; young bark peels away from tree

base of tree swells

Giant Sequoia

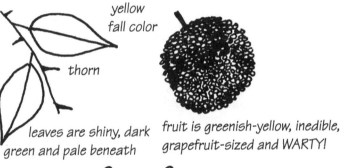

yellow fall color

thorn

leaves are shiny, dark green and pale beneath

fruit is greenish-yellow, inedible, grapefruit-sized and WARTY!

Osage Orange

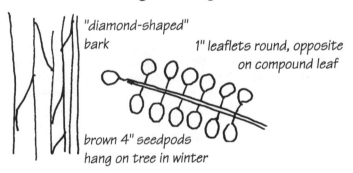

"diamond-shaped" bark

1" leaflets round, opposite on compound leaf

brown 4" seedpods hang on tree in winter

Black Locust

Head toward the path to your left. On the way to the path on the left are two **Giant Sequoias** (Tree 37). These trees once ruled the Sierra Nevada forests at an elevation of about 6000 feet, with 300-foot-plus heights and 30-foot-plus diameters. Climate changes since then have decreased the range of the Sequoias to only 75 groves in Callifornia.

With their dense, lush-looking foliage and symmetrical conical shape, they make a great ornamental tree. Given enough water, they will grow about two feet taller per year. These two trees are probably about 30 years old.

The drawback to planting Giant Sequoias next to your house is that in about 50 years they will dwarf the house. You can see this in Reno, as well as in many cities in the Central Valley of California.

About 200 feet along the path, where it makes a large turn to the right, there is a young tree about 20 feet from the path with sharp spines on its branches. This tree is obviously too hazardous for a street tree, but the spines actually improve its usefulness in certain situations.

This tree is **Osage Orange** (Tree 38 on Map 7), a native of the south-central United States. There it is planted as a hedge tree, because closely-planted trees, with their interlacing branches and thorns, make a formidable barrier to livestock. The fruit is a grapefruit-sized greenish yellow ball with a rough surface like that of a brain; the leaves turn yellow in the fall.

For many years the heartwood, strong yet elastic, was used in the making of hunting bows; the wood doesn't rot easily, so it is used for fence posts.

Flanking the left-hand parking lot ahead is a group of large trees with diamond-shaped bark and compound oval leaves. This tree is **Black Locus**t (Tree 39), a native of the eastern United States planted in many urban settings in the West. In spring it has drooping clusters of fragrant white or pink pealike flowers, which turn into 3-inch brown seedpods in fall. In winter the seedpods hang on to produce interest. Some of the many varieties are thornless.

The tree is used for fence posts, because it is strong and doesn't rot easily. It is one of the most drought-resistant deciduous trees growing in the Intermountain West. Like White alder, it is a nitrogen fixer.

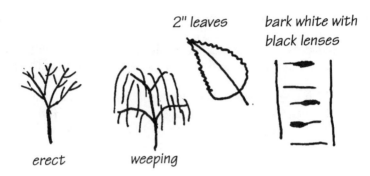

2" leaves

bark white with
black lenses

erect   weeping

European White Birch

10 to 16 leaflets

2" - 4"
leaflets

only desert tree with
reliable fall color

female tree has small
red or black fruits

Chinese Pistache

5"-10" leaves

bark - light green,
mottled, with darker
patches which flake off

fruit-1"
bristly ball

palmate 3-to 5-lobed leaves

London Planetree

Black Locust has another feature which may not be good: it sprouts profusely from the roots, and so it is difficult to eradicate.

The two trees with white bark in this area are **European White Birch** (Tree 40). One of the hardiest of all trees in Europe (it is the last tree seen below treeline in some places), it is an important timber tree there.

In the United States it has a different use, ornamentation. The tree with drooping branches would be called "Weeping Birch"; the other has more upright branches. This demonstrates that two trees of the same type can have a different appearance though growing in similar conditions.

About 100 feet away, in the middle of other trees, is the Nevada Champion **Chinese Pistache** (Tree 41). A native of China, this tree is popular in urban settings because of its color — in spring the new leaves are pinkish, in summer the leaves are bright shiny green, and in fall the leaves turn an orange red (this is the only tree adapted to desert conditions which will reliably give beautiful fall colors).

This tree is in the same genus as the tree which yields pistachio nuts; this tree's nuts have a green flesh inside purple or red 1/4 inch berries.

The two silvery evergreens across the street are an example of how trees can change with age. These are **Colorado Blue Spruce** (Tree 10), just like that beautiful Christmas tree we saw near the beginning of the walk. These two trees likely also had a beautiful conical form many years ago, but with time they have become more craggy. This is something for the tree-lover to contemplate: how will that little Christmas tree look years from now?

Next to the lake near these two trees are specimens of **London Planetree** (Tree 42). They are a hybrid between Oriental Planetree and the American Sycamore frequently seen along city streets.

This hybrid was developed about 1700 in Europe. It has mottled bark and a dense crown of large maple-shaped leave which provides great shade, but it has one undesirable feature: the quite numerous seed balls make a mess for someone to clean up. Many people are allergic to debris from the seed balls and sawdust from its wood.

distinctive drooping twigs
with green leaves

glossy green leaves
3" x 1 1/2"

one of first trees to
leaf out in spring

Weeping Willow

Along the lakeside are three specimens of the last tree on this tour, **Weeping Willow** (Tree 43), a very popular tree around lakes, where its hanging branches add grace to the view (especially in spring, when they are among the first trees to leaf out). A native of China, this tree is now planted all around the world. This was the tree growing in one of the Seven Wonders of the Anicent World, the Hanging Gardens of Babylon.

This tree has some of the same undesirable features as Silver Maple. It is a water-loving tree. This means that if it were planted along a street it would soon destroy water and sewer mains. The branches are brittle like Silver Maple's and break during storms, making a mess to clean up. This tree is host to several insects and diseases, and the three trees along the lake, though relatively young, show signs of these infestations.

This ends our tour. We have seen great beauty — flower color in spring and summer, leaf color in fall, seedpod color in fall and winter, and lovely tree shapes. We have also come to know some of the reason particular species are either desirable or undesirable for planting in yards, along streets, or in parks.

ADVENTURE 7

A Hike to Vikingsholm

This Adventure is a showcase of trees and shrubs which thrive in moist climates. It starts at the Vikingsholm parking lot on California 89 8.8 miles north of the South Lake Tahoe "Y" and 18.7 miles south of the Tahoe City "Y" (see the map in the Foreword for orientation). As with other Adventures, highlighted species are sketched.

As you leave the parking lot, walk to the solitary gnarled tree about 200 feet down the path and 50 feet to the right of the path. This tree, about 40 feet tall and three feet in diameter, has a dead top and dark green foliage only on the lower half of the tree. The Tahoe native Sierra Juniper grows on windswept, dry rocks; frequently it has a gnarled, twisted appearance like this tree's. Note that about half the bark is missing; the remaining bark is fibrous and cinnamon-brown like Incense Cedar's. The vertical lines (about 50 per inch) on the gray bare wood are rings. This ring spacing implies very slow growth. This tree and others like it are something special: they are extremely old. This is the oldest tree you are likely to see in these Adventures; it is at least 1000 years old, possibly 2000 years old.

Sierra Juniper seems to grow where nothing else will, and the best words to describe it are "dogged determination." This tree's trunk, twisted by centuries of icy winds and driving snow is almost stripped bare of bark. Some limbs have been broken off, yet there is a small amount of foliage on them. This tree is an ironic contrast to the scene ahead, a path lush with plants pampered by Nature.

Some of the foliage looks different; it is **Mistletoe**. Although Mistletoe is a good excuse for stealing a kiss at Christmastime, its real purpose is more sinister. It is a parasite, burrowing into the inner bark of living trees and stealing their nourishment. Yet Mistletoe rarely kills its host tree.

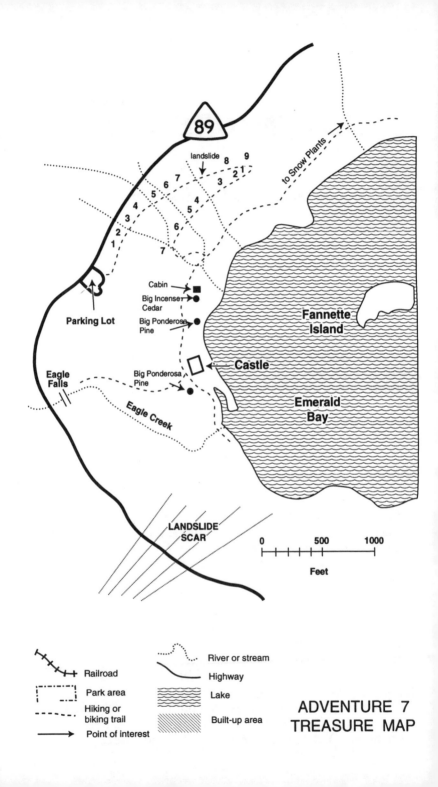

89

landslide

8 9
7   3 2 1
6
5
4   5 4
3   6
2   5
1   6
7

to Snow Plants

Parking Lot

Cabin
Big Incense
Cedar
Big Ponderosa
Pine

Eagle
Falls

Big Ponderosa
Pine

Castle

Eagle Creek

Fannette
Island

Emerald
Bay

LANDSLIDE
SCAR

0   500   1000

Feet

Railroad

Park area

Hiking or
biking trail

Point of interest

River or stream

Highway

Lake

Built-up area

ADVENTURE 7
TREASURE MAP

bluish gray needles and twigs

branching pattern

twigs have diamond pattern

Sierra Juniper

this type grows on
Sierra Juniper

attaches itself to branches
of host tree

Mistletoe

There are four native Sierra Nevada mistletoe species. Two other similar-looking species infest the pines and Incense Cedar.

The hiking path is the road once used by guests of Vikingsholm Castle, a mansion built in the style of a Viking castle. Mrs. Lora Knight, who had Vikingsholm built in 1929, spared no expense. An example of the extravagance is the granite culverts placed along this road; the first of 16 is a few feet past the trail bend to the right ahead of you.

Why so many culverts? There are many small streams descending the steep mountainside, with water seeping into them from the rocks. The rocks above us are fractured, and water from snow melting in the Desolation Wilderness across the highway forms springs above us. They are moist most of the year, one feature which makes this mountainside unusual around Tahoe. In spring and early summer the amount of water in these streams is so great that the road would wash out in several places if there were no culverts.

For us there is another purpose for these culverts: they are landmarks for plants on this hike. For example, there are several kinds of flowering plants near the first culvert: **Lupines** are members of the Pea Family which help other plants because they work in concert with bacteria to store nitrogen (one of the main ingredients of fertilizer) from the soil. **Thimbleberries** have soft maple-sized and -shaped leaves, and also have edible berries. **Bracken Ferns** are common in Sierra meadows. Near the second culvert is **Red Columbine**, the state flower of Colorado; native Sierra Nevada columbines are only red-orange or yellow, but cultivated varieties have many colors.

On the left a few feet before the second culvert are 20-foot shrubs or small trees with multiple trunks. **Mountain Alder** is one of three alders found in California, Oregon and Washington. Red Alder is an important timber tree in coastal mountains; White Alder is common along Sierra Nevada streams below this elevation, but not common here; Mountain Alder is the most common alder at Tahoe. Unlike most other broadleaved trees, alders have woody cones. These hang onto the tree all winter, giving winter interest.

Mountain Alder is usually a shrub rather than a small tree like these; it's just that conditions are optimum for Mountain Alder growth at Vikingsholm.

So what is the difference between a tree and shrub, anyway? There are several definitions, but I prefer the definition established by the American Forestry Association. The AFA defines a tree as a plant growing to 12 feet or more, with one trunk larger than 9 1/2 inches in circumference (essentially 3 inches in diameter) at 4 1/2 feet above the ground; a shrub is shorter with multiple trunks coming out of the ground. Do you think these are shrubs or trees? You will have plenty of opportunities to decide; Mountain Alders are found along this road all the way to the Lake.

1 1/2" leaves

flower panicle is cylindrical
(size 2" X 3"-12") with blue to purple
petals in late spring or summer

view of leaves from top

Lupine

6 " complexly-toothed leaves
have a surface that is rough and
hairy yet soft surfaced

no thorns

Thimbleberry

1'-2' fronds
turn brown and
wither in late summer

branches ("fronds")
almost horizontal

Bracken Fern

doubly lobed leaves

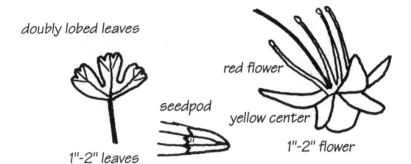

red flower

seedpod

yellow center

1"-2" leaves

1"-2" flower

Red Columbine

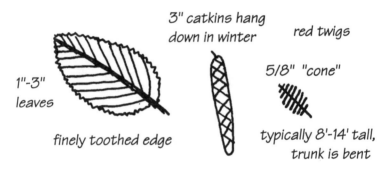

3" catkins hang
down in winter

red twigs

1"-3"
leaves

5/8" "cone"

finely toothed edge

typically 8'-14' tall,
trunk is bent

Mountain Alder

thorny stems

round fruits
("rose hips")

finely-toothed 1"
compound leaves

1" flowers pink,
usually 5 petals

California Wild Rose

Between the third and fourth culverts, and also further down the trail, is **California Wild Rose**. It is easily identifiable as a rose, with its thorns, rose-like flowers and "rose hips" (seedpods which turn to a beautiful bright red color in fall).

Between the fourth and fifth culverts are two species of oak. On the left of the path is **Huckleberry Oak**, common around the Lake and considered one of the main Mountain Chaparral species (we'll see other species in a few minutes); a shrub with hard, dark, yellow-green leaves, it is best identified in autumn and winter when its acorns are ripe. On the right of the path is **Canyon Live Oak**; a medium-sized tree with hard, dark, glossy leaves, it is common in sunny areas on the western slope of the Sierra, but it is out of its range here; I suspect that this group of trees was planted as a landscape planting; an examination of rings on severed branches shows that the trees could be about 70 years old. Canyon Live Oak was important for early settlers; though the grain was too twisted to be useful as lumber, the wood was both hard and durable, and was used for wood-splitting wedges.

On the left just below the sixth culvert is a shrub with red branches, **Creek Dogwoo**d. A member of the same genus as Flowering Dogwood of the eastern U.S. and Pacific Dogwood of lower Sierra Nevada elevations. In spring it has umbrella-shaped clusters of small white blossoms; in fall it has pink, orange, red or purple leaf colors and 1/4 inch berries where the flowers were; in winter red or maroon branches provide color.

When you are halfway between the sixth and seventh culverts, look up on the hillside. To your left are large trees, to your right are large trees, but between them the only trees are small Jeffrey Pines. This is the path of a landslide in 1980, which removed both soil and big trees.

After the landslide, small flowering plants appeared; next, shrubs of an assemblage called "Mountain Chaparral" took over. Besides Huckleberry Oak, there are other shrubs present at Vikingsholm: **Manzanita** has purplish or brownish twisted bark and rounded leaves with pointed ends. **Snow Brush** is the shrub with whitish green leaves and pointed spines. **Bitter Cherry** is the treelike shrub with white almond-scented flowers in late spring, 1/4 inch red fruits in fall which taste bitter to humans (although animals relish them) and reddish bark with horizontal lines typical of cherry trees.

Gooseberries and **Currants** are two types of shrubs in a genus with nine difficult-to-distinguish species in the Sierra

Nevada. Both have tasty berries; gooseberries are covered with thorns for protection from browsing animals, but currants arethornless. Gooseberrries are an intermediate host for White Pine Blister Rust, a disease which has destroyed thousands of

edges of 1" leaves may be smooth or spiny

low shrub (2'-4' tall)

leaves gray-green above, paler below

Huckleberry Oak

some leaves stay all winter

mature acorn is 1 1/2" long

1"-2" leaves, shape varies - smooth to pointed

leaves dark green on top, white on bottom, "hard"

Canyon Live Oak

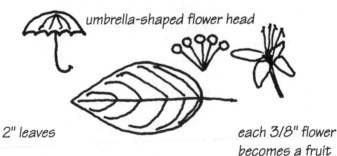

umbrella-shaped flower head

2" leaves

each 3/8" flower becomes a fruit

Creek Dogwood

leaf shape variety

bark is smooth and brown to purple

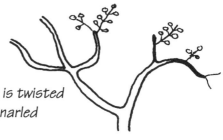

1"-2"
leaves

trunk is twisted
and gnarled

Manzanita

many dead
branches

rounded 1" leaves are light
green above, whitish below

1/8" 5-pointed flowers in
umbrella-shaped clusters
(May-July)

whitish bark

3/4" spines

Snow Brush

1"-2" finely toothed leaf

1/4" bright red
fruits (early fall)

pretty, white,
almond-scented
1/2" flowers in spring

Bitter Cherry

acres of white pine trees. A few decades ago, a concerted effort was launched to eradicate these plants.

What will happen to this landslide area in the future? In the best of all situations, the forest trees would eventually take over. But there are three situations in this place which might prevent that. The first situation is more landslides. The slopes in this area are unstable because the mountainside is so steep, and the rocks are fractured at almost the same angle. Add the pressure of deep snow and ice, and you have essentially a large coaster sled.

The second situation is poisoning of the competition. Many chaparral plants manufacture substances toxic to other plants.

The third situation is fire. A forest fire would be easy to start here: rather than having to leap 60 feet to reach the first branch of mature conifers, a fire can burn the dead branches of typical chaparral plants near ground level. Also, chaparral shrubs are commonly filled with flammable materials. Most of the fires in California start in Foothill Chaparral or Mountain Chaparral.

Fifty feet below the 7th culvert is Snow Brush, one of the 11 species of the Ceanothus genus. Ceanothus is one of the most common plants in the Mountain Chaparral assemblage. As a group, these plants are generally low-lying shrubs with multiple stiff branches, hard leaves, and deep root systems. They are adapted for dry conditions.

The path turns sharply to the right after the 9th culvert. On the inside of the turn is an **Apple** tree. Probably planted to provide guests with spring color, it is now an old, almost dead tree with horizontal lines of holes all over its trunk. These holes were drilled by woodpeckers searching for tasty insects, and the number of holes indicates how bad the tree's health is.

On the right fifty feet past the first culvert after the turn is **Sierra Coffeeberry**, a shrub most noticeable in fall, when its telltale two-lobed, 1/2 inch berries ripen to a black color. The bark of this shrub was used by Indians as a laxative.

Common Mullein is past the third culvert on the right. It has thick, velvety gray-green pointed leaves, and as the summer progresses it sends out a vertical spike up to six feet tall with yellow flowers. This shrub is not native; it was probably introduced through the digestive tracts of the livestock brought in by early settlers. Nevertheless, it thrives here and will crowd out lessaggressive plants. The National Park Service is trying to eradicate it in Yosemite Valley, but it is so tenacious and common that its eradication is unlikely.

small, indistinct flowers

1/4" berry has two lobes,

very finely toothed
2"-3" leaf

may be either tree or
shrub; crooked trunk

Sierra Coffeeberry

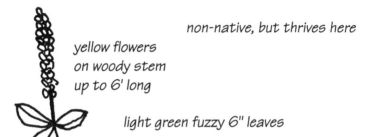

non-native, but thrives here

yellow flowers
on woody stem
up to 6' long

light green fuzzy 6" leaves

Common Mullein

Where the road turns sharply to the left, look at the cliff ahead of you. About 200 feet high, it is part of the Vikingsholm Tree Story. Have a seat at one of the benches past the turn, under the trees with smooth gray trunks and initials carved in them. These trees are **Scouler Willow**, the only easily-identifiable of the 14 plus willow species. There are three reasons for this easy identification: first, Scouler Willow leaves are not long, thin and pointed like those of other willows, but instead are short and broad; second, the leaves are widest more than halfway from the twig end; third, they are the only willows which prosper on dry hillsides (although this hillside is moist). It is difficult for me (and apparently even botanists) to differentiate between the species, so for convenience I separate willows, Zen-like, into two groups: Scouler Willows and **Not Scouler Willows**.

The biggest Scouler Willows I have seen at Tahoe are at Vikingsholm; and there are huge trees of two other species (Ponderosa Pine and Incense Cedar) in the area around the Vikingsholm Castle. Why?

Let's contemplate. What would be the best growing conditions for trees in the Sierra? They would need a sunny exposure for optimum photosynthesis; abundant moisture most of the year; protection from icy winds which could damage trees by breaking branches; protection from lightning; no removal of the biggest trees by logging; and a deep snow cover to protect the roots.

The eastern and southern exposure here provides plenty of sun; the Desolation Wilderness above us is a very snowy place; the cliff provides a wind shadow in this area; the nearness of the cliff tends to keep lightning away; this area was not logged; and the wind blows protective snow over the cliff. So conditions here are optimum for giant tree growth.

Walk 150 feet to where the road splits. To the left is a service road leading, after about a half mile, to the only boat campground at Tahoe; access to this campground is by boat or foot only. Past it, along the shoreline, is the Rubicon Trail. If you are here in early June, take this trail to see **Snow Plant**. Snow Plant is a saprophyte — that is, it does not photosynthesize like other plants but instead steals its nourishment from other plants. It emerges from the ground looking like a fat, brilliant red asparagus. Other places have scattered Snow Plants, but hundreds of them are visible from the Rubicon Trail when you near Emerald Point. I did not enclose a sketch of this plant because you'll know it when you see it.

If you don't want that extra hike, take the asphalt path to the right. As you head toward Vikingsholm, notice that the Scouler Willow in front of you is 60 feet tall and over one foot in diameter; it has an optimum location next to a stream.

In the clearing, next to the cabin, is the biggest **Incense Cedar** I have seen at Tahoe. It is 8.8 feet in diameter at 4 1/2 feet and 165 feet tall. Walk around this giant tree; one side has bricks. This tree was probably bricked for two reasons: first, the base was at least partly hollow (probably from a forest fire), and the owner wanted to protect the tree. As we know, the center of the trunk is heartwood, which is not alive and is not necessary for survival of the tree; many hollow trees survive. But a hollow tree is weak structurally, because the heartwood supports the tremendous weight of a tree like this. Those bricks may be supporting some of the tree's thirty or forty tons of weight.

About 50 feet from the Incense Cedar in the direction from which you came is a Jeffrey or Ponderosa Pine stump. When cut down, this tree landed on top of a shed; judging from the size of the stump, the building probably did not slow down the tree's fall much. This is one of the most unusual stumps I have seen at Tahoe. The rings are unlike the concentric rings of most pine stumps; the mushroom-shaped groups of rings perhaps indicate that the tree was wounded in several places. The tree grew wood around the wounds to protect the tree from insects or disease. Also, unlike most of the stumps around here, the latewood of this tree is almost as wide as the earlywood.

Continue down the asphalt path 200 feet or so; the huge Jeffrey Pine with old-age bark 50 feet to your left is actually a **Ponderosa Pine**, one of two giants here at Vikingsholm (hint: if old trees have yellow bark plates, they are Ponderosa Pines). It is bigger than it looks from here; you can see how big by standing next to it. It is the biggest Ponderosa Pine in the Lake Tahoe Basin. Ponderosa Pine is found at Tahoe only within a hundred feet or so vertically from Lake level; these two trees and the two trees in this Adventure, near Lake level, are the biggest around the Lake.

The asphalt path continues to the back of the mansion. Go through the doorway into the atrium. The shrubs on the edges of the atrium are **European Mountain Ash**. This nursery shrub has features in common with Sitka Mountain Ash, a Sierra Nevada native: both have yellow berries in summer, which turn orange or red in fall (joined by brilliant orange foliage) and often hang on through early winter to provide cheery color. The difference in the species is availability: European Mountain Ash, sold in local nurseries, is found all around the Lake, but the local native is found nowhere along highways at the Lake. To see the native in its autumn glory, hike Bayview Trail (at mile 7.7 of Adventure 2) during October; where the trail disappears near the rounded granite knobs, look for orange color along the stream.

The undefiled White Fir trees in the atrium, predating the house, show what was foremost on the mind of the architect for the Vikingsholm Castle: to build a replica of a Viking castle without disturbing a single one of the magnificent trees in the area. Mrs. Knight, seeing the fjordlike character of Emerald Bay, wanted an appropriate residence. She went to Scandinavia — including such places as Stockholm, Sweden and Lillehammer, Norway (site of the 1994 Winter Olympics) — to get ideas for a house which would fit well in such a setting. Captivated by tenth to fifteenth century Scandinavian architecture, she had Vikingsholm built.

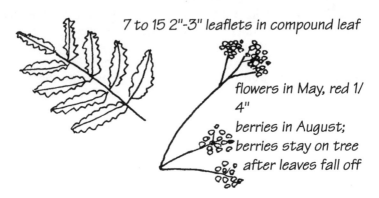

7 to 15 2"-3" leaflets in compound leaf

flowers in May, red 1/4"

berries in August; berries stay on tree after leaves fall off

European Mountain Ash

If you are here between July 1 andLabor Day you can tour the Castle, which features both authentic Viking furniture and cleverly crafted fakes. Even if the house isn't open, the State-tended flower gardens in front of the house contain many beautiful garden varieties.

A marked trail leads in a few minutes to Eagle Falls, the only waterfall visible from the Lake. If you are here in late springorearly summer, the cascading water is beautiful.

Next to the trail, with a dirt path around it, is the widest Ponderosa Pine of Tahoe (7.2 feet in diameter). The bark of this giant is especially picturesque.

As you go around the house and toward the beach, look up to the right at the 1953-55 landslide scar. Much larger than the landslide which crossed the path above you, this landslide was so devastating that there is essentially no vegetation even after so many years. Below the bare area are willows, Quaking Aspens and Mountain Alders, which soak up the moisture permeating through this bare area.

Head back on the asphalt path; when you see the bricks in the huge Incense Cedar, you will see the cliff in another perspective. The walk is steep and the elevation gain is about 400 feet, so take your time and enjoy the beautiful trees, shrubs and flowers!

ADVENTURE *8*

Outstanding Tree Stands

Many tree and shrub species in the Truckee River Basin are well-developed for one reason or another in certain places. If you choose to do this Adventure, you will enjoy magnificent individuals of the species below. If you want to see the biggest of any particular species, go to Adventure 9.

There are two ways to enjoy this Adventure. If you want to look at certain trees or shrubs, look below at the listing for each species; locations are in parentheses. If you want to look at trees or shrubs in a certain area, refer to the map on the next page, keyed to the symbols in the list below.

American Elm (ae) — Along Latimore Drive in Idlewild Park (Adventure 6)

Basin Sagebrush (sb) — At the Nevada 28 vista point (mile 4.9 of Adventure 3);

Bitter Cherry (bc) — On the Vikingsholm trail (Adventure 7)

Bitterbrush (bb) — At the vista point on Nevada 28 (mile 4.9 of Adventure 3)

Black Cottonwood (bc) — At the intersections of California 89 with Ward and Blackwood Creeks (miles 22.7 and 26.7 of Adventure 2); along other creeks, swampy areas and on the upper parts of beaches

Black Locust — (bl) Near the parking area in Idlewild Park (Adventure 6)

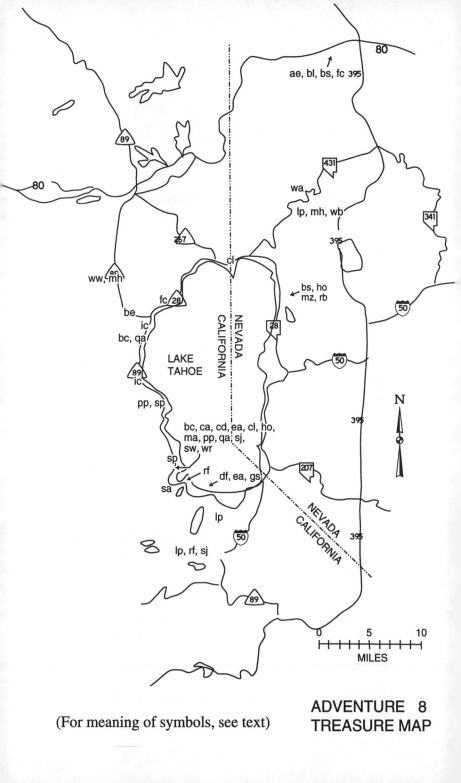

ADVENTURE 8
TREASURE MAP

(For meaning of symbols, see text)

Blue Elderberry (be) — Between the bike path and the Truckee River on California 89 between Tahoe City and Truckee there are three bushes (about mile 11.0, Incline Village to Reno segment of Adventure 5)

California Wild Rose (cr) — On the Vikingsholm trail (Adventure 7)

Canyon Live Oak (cl) — On the Vikingsholm trail; at the Cal-Neva in Crystal Bay (mile 11.2 of Adventure 3)

Colorado Blue Spruce (bs) — In Idlewild Park (Adventure 6)

Creek Dogwood (cd) — On the Vikingsholm trail (Adventure 7); on any creek bank

Curl-leaf Mountain Mahogany — In the Truckee river Canyon from miles 17.0 to 23.0 of the Reno to Truckee segment of Adventure 5

European Mountain Ash (ea) — Inside the Vikingsholm Castle atrium (Adventure 7); in the Tallac Historic Site Arboretum (Side Trip A)

Fremont Cottonwood (fc) — In front of the Watson Cabin in Tahoe City (Adventure 3); in Carson Valley along U.S. 395 from Nevada 431 to the outskirts of Reno (miles 25.1 to 27.1 of the Incline Village to Reno segment of Adventure 5); in Idlewild Park (Adventure 6)

Giant Sequoia (gs) — At the Tallac Historic Site Arboretum (Side Trip A); also visible from the U.S. 395 in Reno

Huckleberry Oak (ho) — At the vista points at miles 4.9 and 17.8 of Adventure 3; on the Vikingsholm trail (Adventure 7)

Incense Cedar (ic) — In three areas along California 89 from Homewood to Tahoe City (miles 20.4 to 27.4 of Adventure 2); also around Vikingsholm Castle (Adventure 7)

Jeffrey Pine (jp) — Along Alpine Meadows Road (mile 9.5 of the Truckee-Tahoe City segment of Adventure 5); look anywhere else in the Lake Tahoe Basin below 7600 feet, although the areas of the state parks are best because they tend to have more old-growth stands

Lodgepole Pine (lp) — Along Nevada 431 from Diamond Peak Cross Country Ski Area to East Bowl of Mount Rose Ski Area (miles 5.2 to 11.8 of the Incline Village to Reno segment of Adventure 5); in Washoe Meadows State Park (see Adventure 9 for directions)

Manzanita (mz) — No outstanding trees, but present everywhere; at the vista points at miles 4.9 and 17.8 of Adventure 3

Mountain Alder (ma) — On the Vikingsholm trail (Adventure 7)

Mountain Hemlock (mh) — Along Nevada 431 from Mount Rose Summit northeast about 1/2 mile (miles 8.3 to 8.8 ofthe Incline Village to Reno segment of Adventure 5); visible from the Squaw Valley Tram about 1/2 way up, looking to the north

Ponderosa Pine (pp) — Near Vikingsholm Castle (Adventure 7); along the shoreline in Sugar Pine Point State Park (mile 17.4 of Adventure 2)

Quaking Aspen (qa) — At the intersections of California 89 with Ward and Blackwood Creeks (miles 22.7 and 26.7 of Adventure 2); along Nevada 431 near the turnoff for the East Bowl of Mount Rose Ski Area (mile 11.8 of the Incline Village to Reno segment of Adventure 5)

Rabbitbrush -(rb) - At the Nevada 28 vista point (mile 4.9 of Adventure 3)

Red Fir (rf) — Along Nevada 431 from Diamond Peak Cross Country Ski Area to East Bowl of Mount Rose Ski Area (miles 5.2 to 11.8 of the Incline Village to Reno segment of Adventure 5); along California 89 near Inspiration Point (mile 7.7 of Adventure 2); on the road to Echo Lake (take U. S. 50 southwest from the South Lake Tahoe "Y" and take the first right after Echo Summit)

Scouler Willow (sw) — On the Vikingsholm trail (Adventure 7)

Sierra Juniper (sj) — On Echo Lake Trail (see Red Fir above), with the best trees past Upper Echo Lake; at the head of the Vikingsholm trail (Adventure 7)

Single-leaf Pinyon (sl) — Along Nevada 341 between U.S. 395 and Virginia City; scarce in the area of Tree Adventures

Sitka Mountain Ash (sa) — On Bayview Trail (mile 7.7 of Adventure 2), along the creek below the rounded granite knobs

Sugar Pine (sp) — On the right side of California 89 at Bliss State Park (mile 10.2 of Adventure 2); near the Lake shoreline north of General Creek in Sugar Pine Point State Park (mile 17.4 of Adventure 2)

Utah Juniper (uj) — Next to the lake on Idlewild Drive, on the south margin of Idlewild Park (Adventure 6); along Nevada 341 between U.S. 395 and Virginia City;

Washoe Pine (wa) — side Trip B; some trees at Galena Creek Park (mile 18.2 of the Incline Village to Reno segment of Adventure 5)

Western White Pine (ww) — On the road from Echo Summit to Echo Lake; on any hike above about 7500 feet; next to "Subway" run in Alpine Meadows Ski Area there is an excellent lone tree; near the tennis courts in Squaw Valley High Camp

White Fir (wf) — Anywhere in the Lake Tahoe Basin below 7000 feet; no outstanding examples of areas

Whitebark Pine (wb) — Along Nevada 431 near the entrance to Mount Rose campground (mile 8.3 of the Incline Village to Reno segment of Adventure 5)

ADVENTURE 9

The Biggest and the Best at Tahoe

This Adventure is about finding the "Biggest and Best" — tallest, widest, oldest and most magnificent — trees of each kind at Tahoe. Below is my own list of these, including directions to find them so you can check them out too. The Treasure Map will help you find them.

How does a tree become the "biggest"? It grew in a spot extremely favorable to its growth, lived longer than the other trees around it, or a combination of both. Not all trees live to a ripe old age; something usually kills them first. I can think of six main things that kill trees, and will apply them to Jeffrey Pines.

The first thing that kills trees is fire, either by burning the cambium (growing) layer or by heating the tree so much that some of the water inside turns to steam and the tree explodes because of the tremendous pressure. For a tree to survive a fire, it has to have wood that doesn't burn readily (like that of Incense Cedar) or bark thick enough to insulate the cambium and sapwood against high temperatures. This means that an old, thick-barked Jeffrey Pine has a better chance of fire survival than the young one next to it; an old tree may have survived many forest fires.

The second thing that kills trees is lightning. A tree taller than any others around it tends to attract lightning, so a tall tree by itself on top of a ridge would probably not get old. Also, there is luck involved; lightning could strike one Jeffrey Pine and not touch one of the same height next to it. (If during your Adventures you see a tree with a vertical line of no bark on the trunk, it's a good bet that the tree was hit by lightning)

The third thing that kills trees is lack of water. A tree with a long tap root going deep into soil would be favored; pines generally have long tap roots, except that many of the pines growing in the deep soils common at Tahoe never develop this

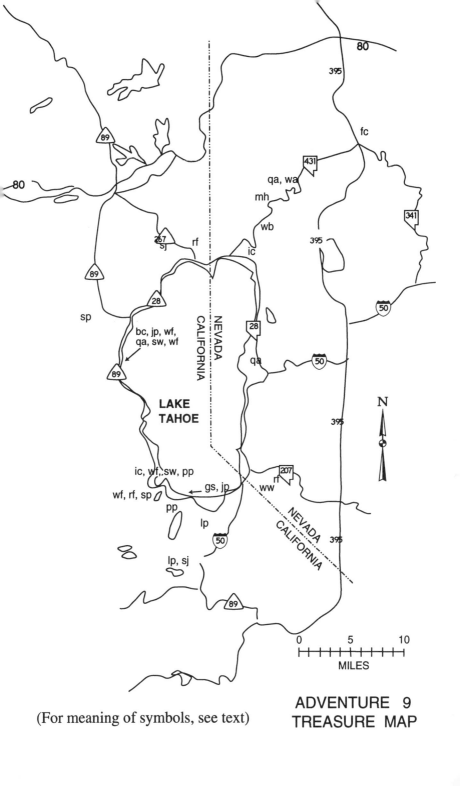

80

395

fc

89

431

qa, wa

80

mh

wb

341

267
sj

rf

ic

395

89

50

28

sp

28

bc, jp, wf,
qa, sw, wf

qa

50

NEVADA
CALIFORNIA

89

N

LAKE
TAHOE

395

ic, wf, sw, pp

207

wf, rf, sp

gs, jp

ww

rf

pp

NEVADA
CALIFORNIA

lp

395

50

lp, sj

0   5   10

89

MILES

(For meaning of symbols, see text)

ADVENTURE 9
TREASURE MAP

root. A tree which grew in a soil with little water-bearing capacity might have to dig deeply, and this might insulate it somewhat against drought years.

The fourth thing that kills trees is lack of light. Sunlight provides the energy to make the tree's food, and a shaded tree is unlikely to grow old (Jeffrey Pine seedlings surrounded by tall forest trees have a very low probability of survival). An old tree as tall as those around it would not be at a disadvantage here.

The fifth thing that kills trees is pests. For example, Jeffrey Pine trees weakened by other stresses cannot fend off attacks by bark beetles. In the mid-1990s, there are many dead trees, and most of these were killed by insects.

The sixth thing that kills trees is wind (or snow). Storms from the Pacific Ocean cross the Sierra Nevada Crest, and break limbs or topple trees with their high winds and heavy snow.

Suppose you were looking for giant trees in an area. What criteria would be most important? My criteria are the following: a place with lots of sun, but with some snow coverage in spring so that moisture is available when the temperature is best for photosynthesis; the west side of the Lake would be better, because there is more precipitation there; a tree in a low area could grow taller with less danger from wind and lightning; a mountainside with water seeping through the rocks, or the side of a creek or pond, would be good for year-round moisture.

Vikingsholm fits all these criteria well: its southeast exposure gives it good sunlight, though not optimum, and snow lingers there later than in some other areas; the cliff protects it from wind and lightning; the water seeping out of the rocks provides moisture.

The monarchs on my list have so far withstood all these threats. Although there may be larger trees in the deep forest, all those I selected are easily accessible (that is, within 100 feet from a road or trail); almost all are encountered during one of the Adventures.

Many of these trees are old and have a short life expectancy (think about your maiden aunt, 104 years old; at this moment, how long do you expect her to around?). So some of the trees listed here may be gone by the time you read this book.

I have measured each of these trees for "dbh" (short for "diameter at breast height," obtained by dividing the circumference at 4.5 feet above the ground by pi); height (measured with an

Abney Hand Level, a standard tool used by foresters); and spread (the horizontal extent of the leaves). I measured the age of stumps by ring count.

The American Forestry Association uses a point system in order to determine the "National Champion." for each species. Their formula adds the circumference in inches at 4.5 feet to the height in feet and to one-fourth of the average spread. The points listed for Tahoe and National Champions for each species were obtained by this method.

The map at the beginning of this Adventure shows the Tahoe Champion trees, keyed to abbreviations found below.

Rivalling champion Trees:

Fremont Cottonwood (fc):

Widest, Tallest, Greatest Spread and Most Points: On a farm near the intersection of U.S. 395 and Nevada 431, south of Reno (mile 26.3 of Adventure 5); 8.1 feet dbh, 84 feet tall, 60 foot spread, 403 points

National Champion: Old Fate Mc Cauley Ranch, NM; 12.0 feet dbh, 87 feet tall, 102 feet spread, 566 points

Incense Cedar (ic):

Widest, Tallest, Greatest Spread and Most Points: At Vikingsholm Castle (Adventure 7); 8.8 feet dbh, 165 feet tall, 70 feet spread, 514 points

Oldest Stump: On the north side of Nevada 28 in Incline Village (mile 13.4 of Adventure 3); 650 years

National Champion: Marble Mountains Wilderness, CA; 12.3 feet dbh, 152 feet tall, 49 foot spread, 626 points

Jeffrey Pine (jp):

Widest and Biggest Spread: On the south side of the road leading to Alpine Meadows, 7.1 feet dbh, 80 foot spread, 100 feet tall, 386 points
Tallest, Biggest Spread and Most Points: Where Blackwood Creek intersects the east side of California 89 (mile 22.7 of Adventure 2); 200 feet tall, 30 feet spread, 4.7 feet dbh, 386 points
Oldest Stump: U.S.F.S. Visitor Center (Side Trip A); 340 years

National Champion: Stanislaus National Forest, CA; 8.1 feet dbh, 197 feet tall, 90 feet tall, 527 points

Lodgepole Pine (lp):

Widest, Greatest Spread and Most Points: On right side of Echo Lakes Trail, between Upper and Lower Echo Lakes; 5.1 feet dbh, 60 foot spread, 90 feet tall, 297 points

Tallest: In Washoe Meadows State Park, an undeveloped State Park near the South Lake Tahoe "Y" (from the "Y," drive west on Lake Tahoe Boulevard for about a mile, turning left onto Sawmill Road; across the road from the intersection with Echo View Drive; walk about 200 feet down a dirt jeep path from the road to the edge of the meadow and you'll see it); 100 feet tall, 4.8 feet dbh, 47 feet spread, 292 points

Oldest Stump: Next to Echo Lakes Trail adjacent to Upper Echo Lake; 265 years

National Champion: Winema National Forest, WA; 3.9 feet dbh, 125 feet tall, 53 foot spread, 286 points

Ponderosa Pine (pp):

Widest: Near Vikingsholm Castle (Adventure 7); 7.2 feet dbh, 165 feet tall, 60 foot spread, 451 points

Tallest, Biggest Spread and Most Points: Near Vikingsholm Castle (Adventure 7); 180 feet tall, 70 feet spread, 7.0 feet dbh, 462 points

National Champion: Plumas, CA; 7.6 feet dbh, 223 feet tall, 68 feet spread, 527 points

Quaking Aspen (qa):

Widest: Near the Washoe Pines (Side Trip B); 2.0 feet dbh, 43 feet tall, 18 feet spread, 122 points

Tallest, Biggest Spread and Most Points: Where Blackwood Creek intersects the west edge of California 89 (mile 22.7 of Adventure 2); 100 feet tall, 1.8 feet dbh, 30 feet spread, 176 points

Oldest Stump: On side of trail between Spooner and Marlette Lakes (go ibto Spooner Lake Picnic Area); 90 years

National Champion: Ontonagon, MI; 3.2 feet dbh, 109 feet tall, 80 feet spread, 251 points

Red Fir (rf):

Widest: On the Tahoe Rim Trail near Daggett Pass; 6.5 feet dbh, 20 feet tall (a snag), no spread, 266 points

Tallest: At Bayview Trailhead (mile 7.7 of Adventure 2); 178 feet tall, 4.2 feet dbh, 40 feet spread, 344 points

Biggest Spread and Most Points: Near Snow Lake on Bayview Trail (Adventure 2); 45 feet spread, 5.3 feet dbh, 138 feet tall, 349 points

Oldest Stump: On the Tahoe Rim Trail near Brockway Summit; 370 years

National Champion: Sierra National Forest, CA; 8.5 feet dbh, 180 feet tall, 48 feet spread, 512 points

Sierra Juniper (sj):

(Single trunk)

Widest and Most Points: On Echo Lakes Trail above Upper Echo Lake; 7.4 feet dbh, 42 feet tall, 40 feet spread, 331 points

Tallest: On the Tahoe Rim Trail between Brockway Summit and Watson Lake; 81 feet tall, 6.3 feet dbh, 27 feet spread, 326 points
Biggest Spread: On Echo Lakes Trail above Upper Echo Lake; 45 feet spread, 6.1 feet dbh, 60 feet tall, 300 points

Oldest Stump: On the Tahoe Rim Trail between Brockway Summit and Watson Lake; 500 years

(Multiple trunks)

Widest, Tallest, Biggest Spread, Most Magnificent and Most Points: on Echo Lakes Trail above Upper Echo Lake; 11.3 feet dbh, 66 feet tall, 60 feet spread, 508 points (7 trunks)

National Champion: Stanislaus National Forest, CA; 12.7 feet dbh, 86 feet tall, 58 feet spread, 581 points

Western White Pine (ww):

Widest, Tallest, Biggest Spread, Most Magnificent and Most Points: On the Tahoe Rim Trail, about a two-hour hike south of Daggett Pass; 8.2 feet dbh, 150 feet tall, 60 feet spread, 474 points (This tree is the most magnificent tree I have seen at Tahoe; it has a fallen limb three feet in diameter and awesome bark; it's well worth a hike!)

National Champion: El Dorado National Forest, CA; 10.5 feet dbh, 151 feet tall, 52 feet spread, 558 points

White Fir (wf):

Widest: At Vikingsholm (Adventure 7); 6.4 feet dbh, 50 feet tall (a snag), no spread, 290 points

Tallest, Biggest Spread and Most Points: At Black Bear Tavern on California 89 three miles south of Tahoe City (mile 22.8 of Adventure 2); 150 feet tall, 28 feet spread, 4.9 feet dbh, 343 points; (but its top is dead, so this tree will probably be removed)

Oldest Stump: At Bayview Trailhead (mile 7.7 of Adventure 2); 300 years

National Champion: Omitted from 1992 Register of National Champions, but a tree near Mt. Diablo, CA is 8.8 feet dbh and 179 feet tall (my estimate of points 525)

Not Rivalling National Champions:

Black Cottonwood (bc):

Widest, Tallest, Greatest Spread and Most Points: Where Blackwood Creek intersects the west edge of California 89 (mile 22.7 of Adventure 2); 3.6 feet dbh, 100 feet tall, 32 feet spread and 243 points

National Champion: Willamette Mission State Park, OR, 8.4 feet dbh, 155 feet tall, 110 feet spread, 498 points

Giant Sequoia (gs):

Widest, Biggest Spread and Most Points: In the Tallac Historic Site Arboretum (Side Trip A); 5.9 feet dbh, 110 feet tall, 23 feet spread, 339 points

Tallest: In the Tallac Historic Site Arboretum (Side Trip A); 115 feet tall, 5.3 feet dbh, 27 feet spread, 323 points

National Champion: "General Sherman," in Sequoia National Park, CA; 26.5 feet dbh, 275 feet tall, 107 foot spread, 1300 points

Mountain Hemlock:

(No outstanding trees, but typical trees at Mount Rose Summit are two feet dbh, 60 feet tall, 40 feet spread)

National Champion: Alpine County, CA; 7.3 feet dbh, 113 feet tall, 44 feet spread, 401 points

Scouler Willow (sw):

Widest, Tallest, Biggest Spread and Most Points: On the Vikingsholm Trail (Adventure 7); 1.8 feet dbh, 66 feet tall, 30 feet spread, 140 points

National Champion: Willamina, OR; 6.2 feet dbh, 53 feet tall, 45 feet spread, 297 points

Sugar Pine (sp):

Widest, Tallest, Biggest Spread and Most Points: At the Bayview Trailhead (mile 7.7 of Adventure 2); 6.1 feet dbh, 154 feet tall, 50 foot spread, 396 points

Most Magnificent: Pick your favorite tree alongside California 89 in Bliss State Park

Oldest Stump: A log in the Alpine Meadows parking lot; 380 years (undoubtedly gone by now, but included to show age reached)

National Champion: Yosemite National Park; 9.2 feet dbh, 270 feet tall, 68 feet spread, 635 points

Washoe Pine (wa):

Widest, Biggest Spread and Most Points: In the Washoe Pine area (Side Trip B); 3.6 feet dbh, 76 feet tall, 41 feet spread, 222 points

Tallest: In the Washoe Pine area (Side Trip B); 81 feet tall, 3.3 feet dbh, 30 feet spread, 213 points

National Champion: Modoc National Forest, CA; 5.4 feet dbh, 161 feet tall, 64 feet spread,382 points

Whitebark Pine (wb):

Widest and Most Points: At the intersection of Nevada 431 and the road to Mount Rose Campground (mile 8.3 of Adventure 5); 3.3 feet dbh, 45 feet tall, 23 feet spread, 175 points

Tallest and Biggest Spread: Near the above tree; 57 feet tall, 29 feet spread, 2.7 feet dbh

National Champion: Sawtooth National Recreation Area, ID; 8.8 feet dbh, 69 feet tall, 47 feet spread, 412 points

ADVENTURE *10*

Tree Adventures All Year

Many Tahoe visitors come during June, July and August; but people come here all year. Each month the trees are doing something different: even during the winter months, dormant-looking broadleaved trees are doing something. In this Adventure, we'll look at some things of interest for any month you are here.

January

Typically the Truckee River Basin is covered with snow. Snow in the Sierra is wet, and if it falls with little or no wind, it sticks to tree branches and leaves. If it snows while you are here, you are likely in for quite a treat: Sometimes after an overnight snow, the conifers look like flocked Christmas trees, and the bare horizontal branches of the broadleaved trees have an inch or two of snow on top of them. This spectacle is not only great for photographers, but for anyone with an eye for peace and beauty. Typically after the storm the clouds disappear and the sky and the Lake turn Tahoe Blue once again. This, and the cool crisp air, make you feel great to be alive.

After the sun has worked on the snow for a while, gobs of snow drop off the branches, and you start wishing for another storm.

This is not the month to identify broadleaved trees, because almost none have distinctive appearances. The exceptions are Quaking Aspen and the shrubs Mountain Alder, Creek Dogwood and Scouler Willow. Mountain Alder has tiny "cones" and "caterpillars" in its bare branches; Quaking Aspen has almost-white bark and no "cones;" Creek Dogwood has maroon to red twigs on the end of its branches; and Scouler Willow has yellowish branches. All of these grow along water, so go to one of the beaches or 64 creeks in the Lake Tahoe Basin.

On clear days in winter Mountain Chickadees brighten the day further with their beautiful songs; Steller's Jays are present but their calls are harsh. Squirrels sometimes dash between trees. Coyotes prowl for voles, small rodents which make their homes in moist areas of the forest.

In wet and often snow-covered Idlewild Park, Tree of Heaven, Goldenrain Tree and Honeylocust have seedpods hanging on them all winter, but Idlewild Park is not really enjoyable until March, when the trees start to bloom and leaf out.

February

February is almost like January, except that the "caterpillars" of the Mountain Alders, larger and starting to turn green, are now more obvious than the "cones."

Wind during winter storms breaks off branches, needles and leaves, as well as cones; these can be seen lying under the tree on top of the snow.

A good thing to check out is the area around the base of the trees. There are circles of bare ground around the conifers but no circles around the broadleaved trees in the same area. As I see it, there are three main reasons for this: one, these trees have some photosynthesis during winter, so they are using moisture; two, less snow falls in the circle because the leaves tend to intercept it, and when the snow falls off the branches, it tends to fall outside the circle; three, many conifers have a buildup of debris — needles, branches and cones — around the trunk, so the circle area is higher than the surrounding area.

March

If you compared the buds of various trees in mid-February and mid-March, you would find that they have grown in that month, getting ready to burst forth with flowers or leaves in April.

Snow probably still covers the ground, but there is almost as much rain as snow now. Both these are going to keep moisture in the ground, which will help the trees survive the long dry Sierra Summer.

A few of the Quaking Aspen and willow trees at Lake level have furry gray buds this month; in a couple of weeks the first leaves will appear.

In mid-March some of Idlewild Park's many fruit trees, and within a month most will be in full bloom. Two other trees are blooming: American Elm has tiny yellow-green flowers, and Red Maple has tiny red flowers. Most people don't think of such trees as flowering, but in fact all broadleaved trees bloom each year. These two species are especially conspicuous because very little else is happening. Other trees, however, are showing signs of either bursting into bloom or sending out leaves.

April

The Tahoe trees and shrubs finally made it through winter and many are bursting forth with leaves this month. Everywhere you look there is fresh light green growth. Finally you can identify some trees by their leaves; but bear in mind that the earliest leaves are smaller and maybe slightly differently shaped than later ones.

The leaves popping out of thebranches are not new; they were formed last fall, and now are growing in size. The first leaves of Black Cottonwood trees are yellow because the trees haven't gotten their photosynthesis machines operating fully yet. Pink blooms appear on Manzanita bushes starting in April, as do tiny yellow blooms along the catkins of Scouler Willows. Spring bulbs have sprouted, and some of them, particularly crocus, tulips and daffodils, are blooming.

Idlewild Park has many trees and shrubs flowering this month; some tree or other will bloom until midsummer. New Goldenrain Tree leaves emerge salmon red.

May

This is the first month for wildflowers at Tahoe; the plants with big fuzzy leaves and large yellow flowers are Mule Ears. Trees and shrubs are blooming now, especially Bitter Cherry and planted fruit trees.

This month tiny leaves are coming out of the bare ground, paving the way for flowers in summer; and trees and shrubs are leafing out more.

Conifers also show new growth; it is a lighter green color. Jeffrey Pines are extremely interesting this month, because the new growth is not only up but also out, usually in four directions from the top; by the end of the year these short branches may have grown a foot. New White Fir growth is as bluish-green as Colorado Blue Spruce foliage.

This month you may notice haze in the air and a yellowish powder which gets all over everything. This is Jeffrey Pine pollen, and it falls for a couple of weeks. Since there are so many Jeffrey Pines at Tahoe, since it sometimes rains in May, and since pollen floats, there is usually a thick coating of yellow in areas where water has been trapped and has evaporated (paved areas are good places to look).

This is a good month to visit Vikingsholm; the trail is loaded with lush spring growth and some of the plants are flowering. At Idlewild, some trees reward visitors with gorgeous sprays of flowers.

Bears may make their appearance this month. Yes, there are Black Bears at Tahoe, and they are addicted to junk food such as is found in garbage cans. They will be prowling around until October.

June

This is the height of the wildflower blooming season at Lake level. Blue Elderberry is blooming. The beauty of the flowers helps to offset the discomfort (?) of cloudless warm days and the lack of rain which will last until September or October.

Look at a Black Cottonwood tree this month and you will know why it is called "cottonwood"; the tree sheds large quantities of what looks like cotton. This is to help wind or water disperse the seeds, but it makes a mess around large trees at this point.

July

This month wildflowers are blooming all around Tahoe, from Lake level all the way to tree line. At Vikingsholm, Red Columbine and lupines are blooming. At Idlewild, Goldenrain Tree is blooming.

August

This month fruits and seedpods of Creek Dogwood, Blue Elderberry and wild berries are ripening. Fruits of such shrubs are colorful so that animals can spot them, eat the tasty fruits and disperse the seeds by passing them through their digestive tracts. We humans know when the berries are ripe and tasty by their colors too. Besides, the colors are pleasing to our eyes.

Curl-leaf Mountain Mahogany seeds are prominent this month, looking like hairy curled frog tongues three inches long. Sitka Mountain Ash berries ripen this month, turning coral red. These berries will hang onto the tree until after the leaves fall.

September

Incense Cedar cones are visible on trees now, although they are green. Since these are so small and so few you may have to look under a few large trees to find the cones. They look like miniature fleur-de-lis an inch or less long. The best trees to look at are large trees which are not yet old.

Although many Jeffrey Pine trees have green cones, some trees have opened their cones this month, and winged seeds are twirling downward. There are many seeds on the ground, and by the middle of the month some cones also have fallen. White Fir cones are also turning brown, but instead of falling whole the cones are disintegrating on the tree; cone scales are falling, looking like quarter circles. Incense Cedar cones are turning brown. All the conifer trees have some brown needles this month, leading one to believe that they are "sick;" but it's just part of Nature's grand plan.

Some Quaking Aspen and Black Cottonwood leaves have ugly-looking black and yellow areas, and the leaves are sticky and glossy. While this may appear depressing, it is just the trees going through their cycles, and very few of the trees are actually in trouble. Some of these trees are starting to turn color this month; they are especially pretty at the end of the month on Mount Rose Highway.

Bitter Cherry leaves are also starting to turn this month, and the cherries are red.

October

Congratulations! You are here in the most picturesque and colorful month of the Tahoe year. Every day this month things change. For example, Quaking Aspens, willows and Black Cottonwoods started the month at the height of fall color; as the month progresses more and more of the trees lose their leaves.

Wait a minute, why are these trees changing color, and what is the "right" color? The answer lies in the process of leaf color change. Leaves are green most of the year because the chlorophyll the tree puts into them masks their true color. As fall approaches, the tree starts to kill the cells at the base of the leaf, so the supply of chlorophyll is cut off. With less green to mask true color, the apparent color changes. As this process goes on, the leaf essentially dies of thirst and shrivels. The leaf falls when the connection to the branch is so weak that the branch no longer has enough strength to hold onto the leaf. (That is why a lot of leaves fall when the wind blows: the extra force exerted is enough to break the fragile connection)

Okay, so that explains the yellows and browns. Why do some trees have beautiful oranges and reds? Remember that trees, using energy from sunlight, convert carbon dioxide and water from the air into sugars; these are used by the tree for energy for growth. The more sunlight, the more sugar produced. Certain chemicals in the leaf, in the presence of sugar, may turn the leaf red or orange. As the connection between the leaf and the rest of the tree is being shut down, the sugar stays in the leaf and so does the color.

So you're wanting the most colorful leaves and want to know what type of weather to ask the Weather Genie. The best conditions are cloudless (for a maximum of sunlight energy), warm during the day (for a more rapid energy conversion process), with cool nights (for a slowing of the process at night, when the sugar is supposed to go into the tree). This whole process is also triggered by some daylight length — the tree "knows" when to start leaf color turning.

Different types of trees or even individual trees change color to different colors, different extents, and at different times. For example, Quaking Aspen trees in the same area may be at different stages of color change; this means that the season of color change is more spread out.

Vikingsholm is very colorful this month, but Idlewild is even more so: the yellows of Black Locust Black and Fremont Cottonwood and ten other species of trees are an effective backdrop for the blazing oranges and reds of eight species including maples, Chinese Pistache and sweetgum.

Fish are colorful this month too. Kokanee Salmon are plentiful along the Rainbow Trail of the U.S.F.S. Visitor Center.

There are other things to see this month besides colors. Sugar Pine cones are growing larger, and Western White Pine cones are opening; in a year with lots of cones, these are spectacular sights.

November

By early November, many broadleaved trees have lost most of their leaves. Each time it snows, rains or the wind blows, more leaves flutter to the ground.

Incense Cedar sheds its pollen this month.

Some Idlewild Park trees have lost their leaves by early November, but some trees still have blazing colors.

December

At Tahoe, heavy snows come once again. The colors are gone, but the cones of Sugar Pine and Jeffrey Pine are full-sized. And broadleaved trees and shrubs are dormant once more, wating for spring to burst forth with new growth.

If it's a nice day, visit Idlewild Park for winter interest: Northern Catalpa, Black Locust and Honeylocust pods are hanging from the trees; smaller seedpods hang from the branches of Tree of Heaven, Goldenrain Tree and Green Ash; and spiny seed balls hang from London Planetree and Sweetgum.

Every month at Tahoe is interesting, especially if you are aware of the yearly cycles of the trees and shrubs. It's all part of Nature's grand scheme.

RESOURCES

In Print, At Present for Sale in Local Bookstores

Natural Science:

Alt, D. D and D. W. Hyndman, 1975, "Geology of Northern California," Mountain Press Pub. Co., Missoula, Montana, 249 pp.
— Geology as seen from highways in the Truckee River Basin

Arno, S. F., 1973, "Discovering Sierra Trees," Yosemite Assoc., Yosemite, Cal., 88 pp.
— Identification and description of many trees in this book

Berry, J. B., 1966, "Western Forest Trees," Dover Publications, New York, 238 pp.
— Identification and description of many trees in this book, including their uses

Brockman, C. F., 1979, "Trees of North America," Golden Press, New York, 280 pp.
— Identification and description of almost all trees in this book

Little, E. L., 1980, "Audubon Society Field Guide of North American Trees —Western Region," Alfred A. Knopf, New York, 639 pp.
— Identification and description of almost all trees in this book, with great pictures

Peattie, D. C., 1950, "A Natural History of Western Trees," Houghton Mifflin Company, Boston, 751 pp.
— Identification and description of Western U. S. trees

Peterson, P. V. and P. V. Peterson Jr., "Native Trees of the Sierra Nevada," Cal. Nat. Hist. Guides n. 36, Univ. Cal. Press, Berkeley, Cal., 146 pp.
— Identification and description of Sierra Nevada trees

Ross, J. W., 1988, "Tree Selection Guide for Reno, Nevada," 55 pp.
— Guide for planting trees in Reno; good information on how well they grow in Reno

Schaffer, J. P., 1975, "The Tahoe Sierra: A Natural History Guide to 106 Hikes in the Northern Sierra," Wilderness Press, Berkeley, California, 309 pp.
— A hiking guide with wonderful information about Tahoe natural history

Storer, T. I. and R. L. Usinger, "Sierra Nevada Natural History," Univ. Cal. Press, Berkeley, Cal., 374 pp.
— Gives a review of Geology, Botany, Zoology in the Sierra; good illustrations and descriptions of Sierra trees

Thomas, J. H. and D. R. Parnell, 1974, "Native Shrubs of the Sierra Nevada," University of California Press, 127 pp.
— Description of many of the shrubs in this book

Watts, Tom, 1973, "Pacific Coast Tree Finder," Nature Study Guild, Berkeley, Cal., 61 pp.
— Small, inexpensive book for identifying Sierra trees

Whitney, Stephen, 1979, "A Sierra Club Naturalist's Guide to the Sierra Nevada," Sierra Club Rooks, San Francisco, 525 pp.
— Good overall guide for the ecology of the Sierra Nevada

Other Topics:

1989, "Drive around Lake Tahoe," Windchime Productions, South Lake Tahoe, California
— Audio tape of history and natural science; for the circle drive around around the Lake

Huggins, Ellie, 1992, "What Shall We Do Tomorrow?," (Two Volumes covering both South Lake Tahoe and North Lake Tahoe/ Truckee), Coldstream Press, Truckee, California, 158 pp. and 190 pp. resp.
— Directory of activities available in the Truckee River Basin

Lekisch, Barbara, 1988, "Tahoe Place Names," Great West Books, Lafayette, California, 173 pp.
— Tells history of naming of Tahoe Landmarks

Mc Glashan, C.F., 1880,"History of the Donner Party," Stanford University
Press, Palo Alto, CA, 261 pp.
— First book on the Donner Party tragedy

Mc Keon, O. F., no date, "The Railroads and Steamers of Lake Tahoe," from The Western Railroader, reprinted by the Lake Tahoe Historical Society, South Lake Tahoe, California, 22 p.
— History of trains and boats around Lake Tahoe

Scott, E.B., 1957, "The Saga of Lake Tahoe," Sierra-Tahoe Publishing Co., Crystal Bay, NV, 519 pp.
— Photos and essays about communities around the Lake

Scott, E.B., 1973, "The Saga of Lake Tahoe: Vol. II," Sierra-Tahoe Publishing Co., Crystal Bay, NV, 528 pp.
— Photos and essays about communities around the Lake

Stollery, David J., Jr., 1969, "Tales of Tahoe," Western Printing and Publishing Co., Truckee, CA, 249 pp.
— Anecdotes about life at Tahoe

Stollery, David J. Jr., 1988,"More Tales of Tahoe," 290 pp.
— Anecdotes about life at Tahoe

Strong, D. H.,1984, "Tahoe: An Environmental History," Univ. of Nebraska Press, Lincoln, Nebraska, 252 pp.
— Good history of LakeTahoe Basin; try North Lake Tahoe Historical Society

Triptape, 1992, "Donner Pass: I-80 from the Foothills over the Sierra," Echo Peak Productions
— Audio tape of history and natural science; from Auburn to Truckee

Wilson, Dick, 1992, "Sawdust Trails in the Truckee Basin," Nevada County Historical society, Nevada City, California, 90 pp.
  — Good resource for history of railroads and logging in the Truckee River Basin

Out of Print but Avaliable in Local Libraries

Hayden, Mike, 1971, "Guidebook to the Lake Tahoe Country: Vol 1," Ward Ritchie Press, Los Angeles, 120 pp.
  — Travelogue for Squaw Valley and the North and West Shores of Lake Tahoe

Hayden, Mike, 1971, "Guidebook to the Lake Tahoe Country: Vol. 2," Ward Ritchie Press, Los Angeles, 104pp.
  — Travelogue for Donner Pass, Truckee and the Nevada shore

Tahoe Regional Planning Agency (TRPA), 1970-71 (a series of reports on the Lake Tahoe Basin)
  — Reports dealing with such subjects as climate, hydrology and geology of the Lake Tahoe Basin

APPENDIX A.   Community Demographics

Community	Pop. x1000	Traffic Lights	Length miles	Churches per 1000	Businesses Contr.	Prof.	Tour.	Finan.	Total
SLT-Stateline-Kingsbury	23	20	7.0	23	141	225	417*	115	898
West Shore (MB-Tah-HW)	<1	0	1.5	0	19*	2	17*	10	38
Tahoe City	3	1	0.8	11	101*	66	71	70	308
Carnelian Bay	<1	0	2.4	5	38	6	86*	22	152
Incline Village-Crystal Bay	7	4	1.3	7	51	98*	46	87	282
East Shore (GB-CR-ZC)	<1	1	0.3	2	3	14	12	36	65
Truckee - Donner Lake	10	4	2.2	12	187*	105	64	59	415
Squaw Valley	<1	0	0.5	1	72*	4	24	6	106

Sources: Yellow Pages, Census reports, Chambers of Commerce and observation
Length is of more or less continuous business district
Businesses and churches give an idea of main thrust of community:
Churches and people per church give an idea of permanent resident community
Contractors (e.g. building contractors) gives an idea of construction community
Professional (e.g. architects and doctors) gives an idea of office community
Tourist (e.g. casinos and t-shirt shops) gives an idea of tourist trade
Financial (e.g. real estate and banks) gives an idea of second-home owners

Asterisk gives principal source(s) of business

APPENDIX B

Side Trips

Side Trip A. U.S.F.S. Visitor Center and Tallac Historic Site

This side Trip could take anywhere from one hour to a full day, depending on what you want to see. The whole place is excellently signed, and some buildings are manned during the season the area is open, from May 1 to November 1. The rest of the year the buildings are closed and the ground may be snow-covered, but you can cross-country ski into the area in a few minutes (park by the building about 0.2 mile south of the Tallac Historic Site entrance).

Although there are many things to see here, I'm going to tell you more about a few things I found interesting. I'm not supplying maps because there are excellent signs around the area to help you get around.

Tallac Historic Site

Between 1965 and 1971, the U.S. Forest Service acquired the remains of the three contiguous estates collectively known as the Tallac Historic Site. The first building in this area was built around 1873 by "Yank" Clement, and buildings were built and torn down until the mid-1920s, when the present buildings were all in place. Buildings in place at present include the Baldwin Estate Museum, where you can get information about the area; the surrounding cabins, where art exhibits and workshops are offered during the summer; the Pope House, which is an old house open periodically; and Valhalla, where the annual Valhalla Festival is located and which offers space for events.

The Pope House Arboretum

Like the other estates, this house, built in 1894, changed hands. But around 1910, the Tevis Family createded an arboretum of non-native trees. There are some fine-looking non-native trees here (most of which are important lumber species), and I'd like to give you some additional information about the ones for which there are bronze plaques, plus a couple more.

There is very seldom documentation about dates of tree landscaping, but the house was built in 1894, the arboretum was built later. Building activity in this area seems to have ceased in the mid-1920s, so that would be the latest possible date of planting of the trees. My information is that the pond was built around 1905 to 1910, and from the size of the Giant Sequoias and the Douglas Firs those dates sound reasonable.

The pond, waterfall and arboretum were probably built so that the wealthy landowners could entertain guests. The species of non-native large trees makes me guess that the arboretum planners were from Washington or Oregon and were in the timber business. additional information I have obtained is that the owners of the three estates at Tallac were concerned that no native trees be cut down to provide lumber for the buildings. And the number of old Jeffrey Pine trees in this area indicates that this area was never logged.

An ironic footnote to this story of tree preservation is that, with the stresses produced by old age, drought and Pine Beetle attacks, many trees have died here in the last few years, and the once-dense forest is much more open, with stumps abounding.

Englemann Spruce

This tree grows best in high altitude areas with long, cold winters and short cool summers; notable locations for it are Washington and Oregon on the highest mountains, and Colorado just below tree line. This climax species makes good Christmas trees because of its silvery blue-green foliage. Although its weak, soft wood makes it of limited use as lumber, its resonant qualities make it an excellent choice for sounding boards for pianos and violins.

Western Redcedar

A native of Washington and Oregon, this important lumber tree prefers deep, moist soils, but being fairly drought resistant it can grow in a variety of climates. Another ornamental tree, it is mainly used for building construction — siding, shingles and interiors — because it nails well without splitting.

Most of the houses at Tahoe have exteriors of Western Redcedar; the log-cabin-like siding of the Baldwin House (the large house to the west) is also Western Redcedar.

Red Spruce

This native of New England is one of the most important conifers of the northeastern U.S. Often growing at the edges of streams, this medium-sized conifer (height 60 to 70 feet, diameter 1 to 2 feet) is also used for musical stringed instruments. The wood is also useful for construction lumber and for paper pulp.

Western Hemlock

In the wet areas of the Pacific Coast where it is native, this State Tree of Washington provides browse for deer and elk. It thrives as an understory tree to the huge dominant trees because it is very shade tolerant. Although the small needles are reminiscent of the Coast Redwood, it can be recognized by its drooping top characteristic of Hemlocks.

Because this tree treats well, it is useful for pilings and poles, and can be used for general building construction. But perhaps its finest use is for paper, because its fibers make excellent paper. And because it is resistant to scratching, many gymnasium floors are made of this wood.

Giant Sequoia

The three Giant Sequoias here are the largest in the Lake Tahoe Basin, probably because they were planted early in the twentieth century because they got sufficient light and moisture by virtue of their location near Lake level and their being tended by gardeners.

See Adventure 6 for a description of Giant Sequoia.

European Mountain Ash

Although there is no sign for this tree, there is a really nice one near the top of the waterfall. This shrub grows quickly but does not have a long life expectancy, and it is likely that this specimen was not planted in the original arboretum.
See Adventure 7 for a description of this tree.

Douglas Fir

Although this tree is a Sierra Nevada native, the only trees seen in the Truckee River Basin have been planted here. This elevation is probably too high for Douglas Fir.

Douglas Fir grows quickly, and except for Coast Redwood and Giant Sequoia, it grows to a larger size than any other native North American tree. It grows to its greatest size in the rain forest of the Pacific Coast.

This is the most important timber tree in our country, because it has so many desirable characteristics. The wood is heavy, hard, straight-grained, durable, and nails and paints well. It is also the main ingredient of plywood, and can also be used for paper and particleboard. Douglas Fir Christmas trees are highly prized because of their shape and because the wood is slightly aromatic.

This species is also a botanical odditiy. It is almost like a combination of all other conifers: it has characteristics of pines, firs, spruces, hemlocks and larches. Orginally marketed under the trade name "Oregon Pine," this species has had 20 other common names!

Colorado Blue Spruce

This native of the Rocky Mountains is described more fully in Adventure 6.

Quaking Aspen

This tree is included because there is a plaque for it, but Quaking Aspen is a Tahoe native. See Adventure 2 for a further description.

Evergreen Huckleberry

On the edge of the pond are three Evergreen Huckleberries. It may be that these particular specimens were planted by the U.S.F.S. A Pacific Coast native, this shrub thrives near sea level. But it provides the visitor with color: in spring the flowers are white to pink, and 1/4" berries ripen in June. The green, leathery leaves look good all year.

Oregon Grape

There is no plaque for this shrub, but they are found all around the arboretum. This State Flower of Oregon is a native of lower elevations, but it grows well in a wide variety of growing conditions.

It can be recognized by its leaves, which with their pointed edges look like holly. Small clusters of yellow flowers brighten spring, as do the new spring leaflets, which emerge red or bronze.

Baldwin Casino

Among the buildings which have come and gone on Tallac Historic Site is the most notorious, a casino built by "Lucky" Baldwin, who made some of his money on the Comstock Lode.

Now you'll say, "Wait! Isn't casino gambling illegal in California?" This is true, but this didn't stop this entrepreneur who built an elaborate resort in this area, complete with a no-longer-standing hotel. The casino, built in 1903, was a drawing card for wealthy tourists, and Lucky always seemed to know when to turn the casino into a "respectable" place for the sheriff's visits.

This casino has nothing to do with trees, but I like the humor of the situation, so I'm including it here. To reach it, ask at the Baldwin House how to get there. A sign at the site will give you more information, and you can (like me) reflect on how it must have been in those days.

U.S. Forest Service Visitor Center

From the Tallac Estates the Visitor Center is only a ten-minute walk on a marked trail, but you can also travel by vehicle by exiting the Tallac Historic Site and travelling on California 89 to the next right turn, following it to a parking lot. (However, this will probably take ten minutes too) Although this area has many informative signs and the Visitor Center/bookstore building is usually manned, there are two interesting trails originating from the Visitor Enter about which I would like to share with you.

The first is the Forest Tree Trail. This ten-minute easy walk has signs which explain the life cycle of Jeffrey Pine. It may be more suitable for young children than this book.

The second is the Rainbow Trail. It has well-designed signs all along it which will help you understand the forest and meadows, but two places are of particular interest. When you have descended to the floodplain and have a choice of paths, take the left one to the Stream Profile Chamber. Built under Taylor Creek, it has a glass window with views of native trout and salmon, and in September and October it teems with red-colored Kokanee Salmon; what a treat! Ahead on the path is a bridge with a view of the creek from above, and when the fish are running you can see about one fish per square foot flopping around in the shallow water. Continue on the path until you see some small trees which look like they were cut down by someone with an axe. That "someone" was a beaver, which loves to make dams from the Quaking Aspen trees common in this area. This will also give you an opportunity to look at the rings on the gnawed trees. The rings are indistinct but they are there.

Side Trip B. Washoe Pines

A hundred yards from the highway pavement starts. A few yards before the pavement stops, there is a tree on the left side of the road that looks like a Jeffrey Pine but whose shape is "not quite right," with cones too small for Jeffrey Pine. This tree is a **Washoe Pine**, named for Washoe County; it was first discovered by explorer John C. Fremont in 1844 at Pyramid Lake, about 30 miles northeast of Reno. One of the rarest pines, this species seems to have characteristics in common with both Ponderosa Pine its cone size) and Jeffrey Pine (its vanilla smell); some authorities think that it is a hybrid between these two species.

I have not included a sketch here because this species looks like both Jeffrey Pine and Ponderosa Pine.

Side Trip C. Donner Pass-Truckee

This side trip begins at the intersection of Interstate 80 and California 89 South. Driving time is about an hour, but a tour of Donner Lake Memorial State Park will add a couple of hours. A Treasure Map is enclosed for your orientation.

3.6 (3.6) Donner Lake is in the valley of Donner Creek to the left; we will travel along the north side of the lake later in this side trip. The railroad above the lake is the only one across the Sierra Nevada; more about that later.

8.3 (4.7) Stop at the Rest Area at Donner Summit. Notice that between Truckee and here Lodgepole Pine and Red Fir have replaced Jeffrey Pine and White Fir. Also, trees are sparse on the rounded granite mountainsides. This is glacial terrain; the glaciers were not depositing material as at Verdi but instead were only eroding, and the resultant shallow soil cannot support many trees. The scraping action of ice loaded with rocks created the rounded mountains you can see.

By the way, why is this called "Donner Summit" rather than "Donner Pass?" Generally, "summit" is used to denote the lowest road over a "pass." The thousands of emigrant parties traveling westward near here crossed about a mile south of here at Donner Pass, about changed 150 feet below this elevation. Although twentieth-century planners knew much more about optimum routes than 19th-century pioneers, it still took five years to build the ten miles of Interstate centered here.

11.4 (3.1) Take the Soda Springs-Norden Exit and drive left over the Interstate. This is the road to three downhill ski areas and the largest single cross country skiing area in the world (Royal Gorge has 88 groomed trails with a total of 205 miles). Skiing areas are located here for two reasons: first, snowfall is greater than that at most of the ski areas around Lake Tahoe; second, they are

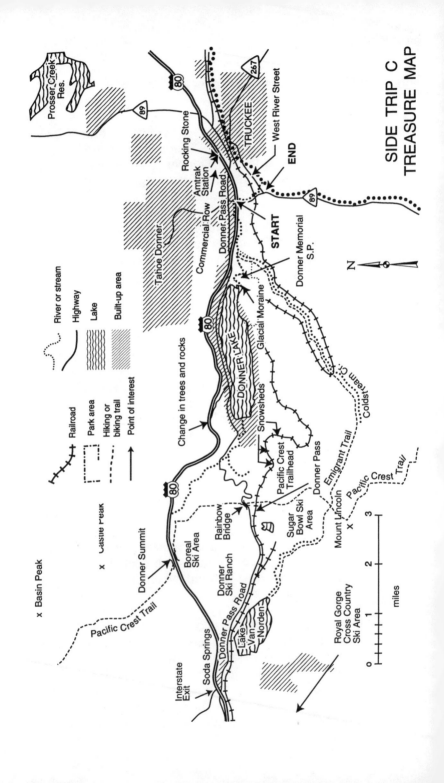

SIDE TRIP C
TREASURE MAP

Legend

- River or stream
- Highway
- Lake
- Built-up area
- Railroad
- Park area
- Hiking or biking trail
- Point of interest

x Basin Peak

x Castle Peak

Prosser Creek Res.

80

89

267

TRUCKEE

West River Street

END

START

Rocking Stone

Amtrak Station

Commercial Row

Donner Pass Road

Tahoe Donner

Donner Memorial S.P.

Glacial Moraine

DONNER LAKE

Change in trees and rocks

Snowsheds

Coldstream Cr.

Pacific Crest Trailhead

Donner Pass

Emigrant Trail

Pacific Crest Trail

Mount Lincoln

x

Sugar Bowl Ski Area

Rainbow Bridge

Donner Ski Ranch

Boreal Ski Area

Donner Summit

Pacific Crest Trail

Interstate Exit

Soda Springs

Donner Pass Road

Lake Van Norden

Royal Gorge Cross Country Ski Area

N

0   1   2   3
miles

closer to Sacramento and the San Francisco Bay Area, home of many Tahoe skiers.

13.3 (1.9) The meadow area in the valley, when filled with water, is Lake Van Norden. Many of the emigrants crossing the Sierra Crest at or near Donner Pass were faced with the grim task of ascending glacial cliffs in terrible weather. Sometimes in order to ascend the wet, slippery cliffs they had to dump all their water and the feed for their animals. After the perilous final push over the crest, they were greeted by this meadow with plenty of water and nourishing grass for their livestock.

15.6 (2.3) Park here in the lot to the right. Congratulations! You are at Donner Pass, the lowest elevation pass over the Sierra Nevada (elevation 7088 feet), and have hardly broken a sweat. Things were not so easy for the Stephens Party, which in 1844 was the first emigrant party to successfully cross the Sierra Nevada (see sidebar).

Things were even rougher for the ill-fated nd infamous Donner Party, which four years later faced death. Although Donner Pass is named for this group, many of the people did not even reach this pass.

Walk toward the mountain. At the bottom of a small hollow, you will encounter a sign at the Pacific Crest Trail. The PCT (see sidebar) extends over 2200 miles from the Washington-British Columbia border south to Southern California, and provides views of many Sierra Nevada peaks. It goes along the west rim of the Lake Tahoe Basin, finally leaving Tahoe at Echo Summit, 9 miles west of the South Lake Tahoe "Y" on U.S. 50.

As you continue on the road, look at the strange rounded topography and contemplate how much trouble it must have been for wagons and people to surmount these rounded obstacles.

It was possibly even more difficult for the railroad. In the 1860s, railroad companies vied with each other to complete the Transcontinental Railroad. Although the Golden Spike was driven in Promontory,

****

The First Crossing of the Sierra Nevada

Much has been wirtten about the ill-fated Donner Party; of the 87 original emigrants in that 1846 wagon train, 40 died. But other many wagon trains successfully negotiated the Sierra Nevada Crest near here without loss of even one life, starting with the Stephens Party in 1844.

The 51-person Stephens Party set out from Council Bluffs, Iowa, in May 1844, not seeking gold (it was not discovered until four years later) but seeking fertile farmland (which they heard was to be found in California). They could not start until May because grass for their livestock would not be ready if they started earlier, but since they had a trek of almost 2000 miles they had to race the Sierra Nevada winter.

After arriving in north central Nevada in October, and having about one month for safe crossing of the Sierra Nevada Crest, they learned from a local Indian chief about a route along a fine river. The river might be fine, but without any roads it was not easy for a wagon train, and winter was fast approaching. At what is now Truckee (named after the chief) the party split up at a river going to the south, with one group with one group staying the winter with six of the wagons, one group attempting the Sierra Nevada crossing at Donner Pass, and one group of six young people on fast horses making a run for it up that river to the south. Every person on that first wagon train survived, and those six people on horses reached a certain 192-square-mile lake after a few miles, rode along its West Shore for a few miles, and crossed the Sierra Nevada Crest, beating out Old Man Winter. They wer the first white people to actually touch Lake Tahoe, although a group led by explorer John C. Fremont had seen the Lake from near Carson Pass a few months earlier.

****

Utah in 1869, the most difficult portion of the rail link — the crossing of the Sierra Nevada — was completed the year before when the Central Pacific Railroad finally laid track to Truckee. The granite wall ahead, and the tunnel after it, were great engineering achievements won with the help of thousands of Chinese coolies. The wall, built without the use of mortar, has been christened "China Wall." See the sidebar for more details.

Rainbow Bridge, about 0.4 miles ahead, is one of the symbols of Truckee. It was completed in 1926 as part of the Lincoln Highway. This road, originally built between 1863 and 1868 as a wagon road to facilitate construction of the railroad, was the main road over the Sierra Nevada Crest until Interstate 80 was finished in 1964.

18.4 (2.8) The road reaches the upstream end of Donner Lake, where Donner Creek is building a delta into the lake. The lake, three miles long and 1/2 mile wide, resulted when the glacier in this valley scoured out a depression. Ice filled the lake and made a terminal moraine across the valley at the other end. When the glacier melted, water filled the dammed depression.

Cold air crossing the Sierra Nevada Crest settles in this valley; as a result, nights at Truckee are often cold. Truckee claims the title of "Coldest Place in the Nation." In the last decade, there has been an informal contest to determine which place in the lower 48 United States has the lowest temperature the most nights of the year. Truckee could not hope to compete with such iceboxes as International Falls (Minnesota) in the winter; but in spring, summer and fall Truckee has the coldest temperature about 30 to 40 nights in an average year, more than any competitor.

21.0 (2.6) Turn right into Donner Lake Memorial State Park. Most families in the Donner Party camped here in the winter of 1848-49. The base of the memorial statue is at the depth of the snow here in that winter, which was one of the snowiest in the area's history. There is much

****

The Rail Crossing of the Sierra Nevada Crest

By 1861, the year the Civil War started, the United States had become a smaller place. The country was moving west, spurred on by Gold Fever, stories of great farming in California valleys and the urge for "elbow room." Added to this was technological advances in rail travel. The idea of a transcontinental rail link had one problem: laying rails across the Sierra Nevada.

An engineer named Theodore Judah surveyed a rail route across the crest of the Sierra Nevada in 1861. "Crazy Judah," as he was termed by non-visionaries, talked four Sacramento merchants (one of whom was Leland Stanford, for whom Stanford University is named) into financing this operation, and the Central Pacific Railroad was born.

At that time, the engineering problems were considered unsurmountable, but American ingenuity and indomitable will prevailed. Construction started in 1863 from Sacramento; by April 1868 the spine of the Sierra was conquered, partly with the help of retaining walls, trestles and tunnels in the more hair-raising portions of the road.

Or was it? Heavy snows in the 30 miles around Donner Pass caused avalanches and rockslides which buried track. The technological answer was the building of snowsheds to protect trains from material moving downslope; wherever there was a risk, a snowshed was built. By 1868, there were 23 miles of snowsheds, 13 of them continuous. But there were two big problems with snowsheds: these wooden structures caught fire, and the burgeoning group of tourist riders couldn't see the picturesque Sierra they were crossing. The fire problem was eventually alleviated by changing the snowshed material to concrete, and the advent of diesel locomotives which don't spew out cinders. The visibility problem was attacked in two ways. Every other board was removed on the downhill side of the snowsheds, and this helped. What helped more was double-tracking: another track was laid outside the snowshed. In summer the passengers had unlimited visibility, and in winter the train could retreat inside the snowsheds.

The invention of the rotary snowplow (for clearing tracks of heavy snow) made it possible to remove all but the four miles of snowsheds seen today along the Sierra Nevada Crest.

****

easily available information about the Donner Party at this park and around Truckee.

About 0.4 miles ahead at the light, you can either turn right onto Interstate 80 East and then take the U.S. 89 Exit to Tahoe City (if so, go to Page 89 of Adventure 5), or you can continue on Donner Pass Road across over Interstate 80 and tour Truckee (for which the road log continues below).

23.3 (2.3) As you cross under the freeway, a left turn on High Street leads to the Rocking Stone; straight ahead leads to the district of Truckee named "Commercial Row." This is the only town in the Truckee River Basin with 19th-century architecture, and some of the historic houses of town have been converted into shops. Because fire has ravaged Truckee many times in the last century, most of the original buildings are gone; some of the old-looking buildings on Commercial Row are well-done reproductions. Truckee is the only town along our Adventure routes with this old-time atmosphere.

The Amtrak and bus terminals are in the old railroad depot. Daily Amtrak trains pass through here at the only stop between Reno (about an hour to the east) and Colfax (about an hour to the west). Schedules are such that you can travel from Reno to Colfax and back the same day, crossing the marvelous Sierra Nevada; but you will need reservations, because this is on the only east-west route through northern California and Nevada. White you are at the train station, check out the bronze E Clampus Vitus plaque (see sidebar for more information about E Clampus Vitus).

24.1 (0.8) Turn right onto California 267, and turn right again onto West River Street. At 25.3, this street intersects with California 89. This is the end of Side Trip C.

****

E Clampus Vitus

There are fraternal organizations all over the world, but one is unique to the Sierra Nevada: E Clampus Vitus. In the California gold country, miners performed backbreaking work every day in hopes of striking it rich. Usually far away from home and friends, they gravitated to fraternal organizations such as the Masons, Odd Fellows and the like. The few who got their big strike were usually quite generous, and freely rewarded their organization with money for building lodges.

Most organizations had secret signs and were serious about their role in society; even today they go about philanthropic work in their communities. But J. H. Zumwalt founded E Clampus Vitus in 1850 with one apparent purpose: to spoof those solemn societies. New members were welcomed gladly, and the initiation rite often consisted of buying a round of drinks for the old members. They would get grand titles such as "Noble Grand Humbug" (no doubt an inspiration for naming the mining town at Malakoff Diggins State Park in Nevada County — which has an E Clampus Vitus Building — "Humbug").

After gold mining languished, E Clampus Vitus went out of existence; but it has been gleefully resurrected in recent years. There are signs of it today; there are actually bronze signs BY it today (at such places as Carson Pass and at the Amtrak station and the Rocking Stone in Truckee), which commemorate the rich history of the area.

****

APPENDIX C

Common and Latin Names

      Different people call the same tree species different common names. The most extreme example of this is Douglas Fir, which has at least 21 different common names! Here is a listing of common names used in this book with their Latin equivalents.

American Elm	*Ulmus americana*
Amur Maple	*Acer ginnala*
Apple	*Malus sp.*
Atlas Cedar	*Cedrus atlantica*
Baldcypress	*Taxodium distichum*
Basin Sagebrush	*Artemesia tridentata*
Bishop Pine	*Pinus muricata*
Bitter Cherry	*Prunus emarginata*
Bitterbrush	*Purshia tridentata*
Black Cottonwood	*Populus trichocarpa*
Black Locust	*Robinia pseudoacacia*
Black Tupelo	*Nyssa sylvatica*
Blue Elderberry	*Sambucus caerulea (* or *glauca)*
Bracken Fern	*Pteridium aquilinum*
Bur Oak	*Quercus macrocarpa*
California Wild Rose	*Rosa sp.*
California Black Oak	*Quercus kelloggii*
Canyon Live Oak	*Quercus chrysolepsis*
Cedar of Lebanon	*Cedrus libani*
Cherry	*Prunus sp.*
Chinese Pistache	*Pistachia chinensis*
Colorado Blue Spruce	*Picea pungens*
Common Hackberry	*Cercis occidentalis*
Common Horsechestnut	*Aesculus hippocastanum*
Common Lilac	*Syringa vulgaris*
Common Mullein	*Verbascum thapsus*

Crabapple	*Malus sp.*
Creek Dogwood	*Cornus stolonifera*
Curl-leaf Mountain Mahogany	*Cercocarpus ledifolius*
Currant	*Ribes sp.*
Dawn Redwood	*Metasequoia glyptostroboides*
Douglas Fir	*Pseudotsuga menziesii*
Eastern White Pine	*Pinus strobus*
Engelmann Spruce	*Picea engelmanii*
European Mountain Ash	*Sorbus aucuparia*
European White Birch	*Betula pendula*
Evergreen Huckleberry	*Vaccinium ovatum*
Fremont Cottonwood	*Populus fremontii*
Fruiting Pear	*Pyrus sp.*
Fruitless White Mulberry	*Morus alba*
Giant Sequoia	*Sequoiadendron giganteum*
Ginkgo	*Ginkgo biloba*
Goldenrain Tree	*Koelreuteria paniculata*
Gooseberry	*Ribes sp.*
Green Ash	*Fraxinus pennsylvanica*
Hawthorn	*Crateagus sp.*
Honeylocust	*Gleditsia tricanthos*
Huckleberry Oak	*Quercus vaccinifolia*
Incense Cedar	*Calocedrus decurrens*
Jeffrey Pine	*Pinus jeffreyi*
London Planetree	*Platanus acerifolia*
Lodgepole Pine	*Pinus contorta (or murrayana)*
Lombardy Poplar	*Populus nigra var. italica*
Lupine	*Lupinus sp.*
Manzanita	*Arctostaphylos sp.*
Mountain Alder	*Alnus tenuifolia*
Mountain Hemlock	*Tsuga mertensiana*
Northern Catalpa	*Catalpa speciosa*
Not Scouler Willow	*Salix sp.*
Oregon Grape	*Mahonia aquifolium*
Osage Orange	*Maclura pomifera*
Pin Oak	*Quercus palustris*
Ponderosa Pine	*Pinus ponderosa*
Purple-leaf Smokebush	*Cotinus coggygria*
Quaking Aspen	*Populus tremuloides*
Rabbit Brush	*Chrysothamnus nauseosus*
Red Columbine	*Aquilegia truncata*

Red Fir	*Abies magnifica*
Red Maple	*Acer rubrum*
Scouler Willow	*Salix scouleriana*
Sierra Coffeeberry	*Rhamnus rubra*
Sierra Juniper	*Juniperus occidentalis*
Silver Maple	*Acer saccharinum*
Singleleaf Pinyon Pine	*Pinus monophylla*
Sitka Mountain Ash	*Sorbus sitchensis*
Snow Brush	*Ceanothus cordulatus*
Snow Plant	*Sarcodes sanguinea*
Sugar Pine	*Pinus lambertiana*
Sweetgum	*Liquidambar styraciflua*
Thimbleberry	*Rubus parviflorus*
Tree of Heaven	*Ailanthus altissima*
Trident Maple	*Acer buergeranum*
Tulip Tree	*Liriodendron tulipifera*
Utah Juniper	*Juniperus utahensis*
Valley Oak	*Quercus lobata*
Washoe Pine	*Pinus washoensis*
Weeping Willow	*Salix babylonica*
Western Hemlock	*Tsuga heterophylla*
Western Redcedar	*Thuja plicata*
Western White Pine	*Pinus monticola*
White Alder	*Alnus rhombifolia*
White Fir	*Abies concolor*
Whitebark Pine	*Pinus albicaulis*
Willow	*Salix sp.*
Wisteria	*Wisteria sp.*

APPENDIX D

Handy-Dandy Tree Identifier

Although at least 42 species of tree and 60 species of shrub are native to the Sierra Nevada, the likelihood of your encountering most of them in these Adventures is extremely small. The Tree Identifer below should help you identify the 19 species of trees and 17 species of treelike shrubs making up about 99.99 percent plus of what you may encounter here.

Please bear in mind that people plant all sorts of non-native species in their yards, so this identifier will only apply to plants away from built-up areas.

Besides a "Tree Key," I'm supplying a table of elevation ranges for the commonest trees and shrubs; so if you have a question about identity, check the elevation range table below the Tree Identifier.

Tree Identifier:

If it is a CONIFER

And has a bunch of cones under it

And has a droopy top it is a MOUNTAIN HEMLOCK

And the needles are in bundles it is a PINE

And there is one needle in a bundle it is a SINGLE-LEAF PINYON PINE

And there are two needles in a bundle it is a LODGE-POLE PINE

And there are three needles in a bundle it is a YELLOW PINE

And the cones are more than six inches long and the bark smells like vanilla it is a JEFFREY PINE

And the cones are less than six inches long and thebark does not smell it is a PONDEROSA PINE

And the cones are less than six inches long and thebark does smell it is a WASHOE PINE

And there are more than three needles in a bundle it is a WHITE PINE

And the cones are about a foot long it is a SUGAR PINE

And the cones are about six incheslong it is a WESTERN WHITE PINE

And the cones are about an inch long it is a WHITE-BARK PINE

And the cones are long, skinny and soft and the needles are bluish and stiff it is a COLORADO BLUE SPRUCE

And there are few or no cones under the tree

And it has upward-pointing cones on the top fourth of the tree it is a FIR

And the needles have a 1/4 twist and are yellow where they join the twig it is a WHITE FIR

And the needles don't it is a RED FIR

And the bark is dark brown to cinnamon with deep vertical ridges (on old trees) or bark you can peel (on young trees)

And the groups of needles are flat, droopy and look like fingers it is an INCENSE CEDAR

And the twigs are barbed it is a GIANT SEQUOIA

And the groups of needles are round it is a JUNIPER

And you are in the Lake Tahoe Basin it is a SIERRA JUNIPER

And you are in the desert it is a UTAH JUNIPER

If it is BROADLEAVED

And it has one main trunk it is a TREE

And its trunk is smooth and white or pale yellow-green

And it is has smooth-edged leaves it is a QUAKING ASPEN

And it has toothed leaves it is a EUROPEAN WHITE BIRCH

And its leaves are smooth, glossy and longer than wide it is a BLACK COTTONWOOD

And its leaves have wavy edges

And its branches all point upwards it is a LOMBARDY POPLAR

And its branches don't it is a FREMONT COTTON-WOOD

And it has many trunks it is a SHRUB

And it is low-lying with many crooked branches

And its leaves are thick and canoe-shaped it is a CURL-LEAF MOUNTAIN MAHOGANY

And its leaves are almost round it is a MANZANITA

And its leaves have three lobes on the end

And they are silvery it is BASIN SAGEBRUSH

And they are green it is BITTERBRUSH

And it has rounded leaves and thorns it is SNOW BRUSH

And it has many trunks reaching upward

And it has some leaves with spines on their edges it is a HUCKLEBERRY OAK

And it has tiny cones it is a MOUNTAIN ALDER

And it has compound leaves

And the leaves are coarsely toothed it is a SITKA MOUNTAIN ASH

And the leaves are finely toothed it is a BLUE ELDERBERRY

And it has simple leaves and colored twigs

And the twigs are yellowish it is a WILLOW

And the leaves are widest toward the end it is a SCOULER WILLOW

And the leaves are widest toward the tree it is a NOT SCOULER WILLOW

And the twigs are reddish

And it has thorns it is a CALIFORNIA WILD ROSE

And it has no thorns

And it has wide 2 to 3 inch leaves it is a CREEK DOGWOOD

And it has narrow 2 to 3 inch leaves it is a SIERRA COFFEEBERRY

And it has smaller leaves
it is a BITTER CHERRY

Elevation ranges of native species in the Truckee River Basin

Native Species   Elevation, Feet

```
                       5000       7000       9000
                        |          |          |
Basin Sagebrush         ---------------------------------
Bitterbrush             ---------------
Bitter Cherry           --------------------
Black Cottonwood        ---------------
Blue Elderberry         ---- - - -
California Wild Rose     ---------------------------------
Creek Dogwood           ----------------
Curl-leaf Mountain
   Mahogany             ------------------
Fremont Cottonwood      ---------
Manzanita               ----------------------------------
Huckleberry Oak         ----------------------------------
Incense Cedar           --------- - - -
Jeffrey Pine            -----------------
Lodgepole Pine          ---------------------------------
Mountain Alder          --------------------
Mountain Hemlock                   ----------------
Ponderosa Pine          ------- - -
Quaking Aspen               -------------------------
Red Fir                        ---------------------
Scouler Willow          ---------------------------------
Sierra Coffeeberry      ---------------
Sierra Juniper                  - - ----------------------
Single-leaf Pinyon Pine        -------------------
Sitka Mountain Ash                 --------------------
Snow Brush              ---------------------------
Sugar Pine              ------------- - -
Utah Juniper                   --------------------
Washoe Pine                 - - ----------------------
Western White Pine             ------------------
White Fir               ---------------- - -
Whitebark Pine                        ---------
```

(Non-native species commonly planted at Tahoe include Colorado Blue Spruce, European Mountain Ash, European White
Birch and Giant Sequoia)

APPENDIX E

Some Mountain Peaks of the Truckee River Basin

The map in this Appendix shows mountain peaks in the area of Tree Adventures at Tahoe. Note that there are three kinds: those that define the Lake Tahoe Basin, those that define the somewhat larger Truckee River Basin (asterisked in the accomanying table), of which the Lake Tahoe Basin is a part; and other peaks of interest in these Adventures (double-asterisked in the table).

For each peak, the elevation and rock type are given.

Number	Name	Elevation	Type Rock
1	Rifle Peak	9450	Granitic
2	Mount Rose	10778	Volcanic
3	Slide Mountain	9694	Granitic
4	Marlette Peak	8780	Granitic
5	Duane Bliss Peak	8658	Granitic
6	Genoa Peak	9150	Granitic
7	Monument Peak	10067	Granitic
8	Freel Peak	10881	Glaciated Granitic
9	Waterhouse Peak	9500	Glaciated Granitic
10	Stevens Peak	10559	Glaciated Volcanic
11	Little Round Top	9590	Glaciated Volcanic
12	Ralston Peak	9235	Granitic
13	Cracked Crag	8782	Granitic
14	Mount Tallac	9735	Volcanic
15	Dicks Peak	9974	Volcanic
16	Rubicon Peak	9183	Dioritic
17	Lost Corner Mtn.	8261	Granitic
18	Ellis Peak	8740	Volcanic
19	Ward Peak	8637	Metamorphic
20	Scott Peak	8165	Volcanic

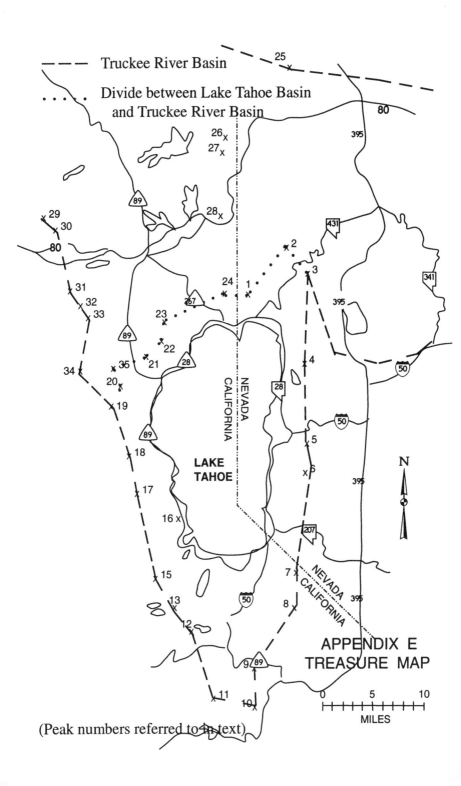

Truckee River Basin

Divide between Lake Tahoe Basin
and Truckee River Basin

APPENDIX E
TREASURE MAP

N

0   5   10
MILES

LAKE
TAHOE

CALIFORNIA
NEVADA

NEVADA
CALIFORNIA

(Peak numbers referred to in text)

Number	Name	Elevation	Type Rock
21	Unnamed	7572	Volcanic
22	Mount Watson	8424	Volcanic
23	Mount Pluto	8617	Volcanic
24	Martis Peak	8656	Volcanic
25	Peavine Peak	8266	Metavolcanic
26	Granite Peak	8291	Granitic
27	Verdi Peak	8444	Granitic
28	Boca Hill	7051	Volcanic
29	Basin Peak	9015	Granitic
30	Castle Peak	9103	Glaciated Volcanic
31	Mount Lincoln	8383	Glaciated Volcanic
32	Anderson Peak	8683	Glaciated Volcanic
33	Tinkers Knob	8949	Glaciated Volcanic
34	Squaw Peak	8895	Glaciated Volcanic
35	KT-22	8070	Glaciated Volcanic

Dimensions of an Old-age Jeffrey Pine

Age: 300 years

Size: Height: 140 feet
     Diameter: 4.3 feet
     Volume: 730 cubic feet
     Weight ("dry"): 8 tons
     Weight ("wet"): 18 tons
(cf. Blue Whale 109 tons, White Rhino 3 1/2 tons)
     Roots: About 1/4 weight of tree
     Total Water Processed through Tree: 1 million gallons
     Inner Bark Volume: 50 cubic feet
     Sugar in Inner Bark: 300 pounds

Leaves: Number: 1 million
       Surface Area: 14,000 square feet (1/3 acre)

Cones: Number Annually: 500
       Seeds: 150 per cone, 75,000 total (7.5 pounds)

Fluids: Root Pressure: 50 psi
      Leaf Pressure: 2000 psi
      Amount: 300 gallons per day

Number of Jeffrey Pines in Lake Tahoe Basin: 9 million

Potential Jeffrey Pine Lumber in Lake Tahoe Basin: 11 billion board feet

Energy Budget:

Transpiration (cooling)	10 %
Repair and Replacement of leaves and roots	35 %
Seed Production	2 %
Adding Wood	53 %
Total	100 %

APPENDIX G

Lake Tahoe Basin Water Facts

	Precipitation on Land	672,000 Acre-feet
minus	Losses from Land	355,000 Acre-feet
net	Inflow to Lake	312,000 Acre-feet
plus	Precipitation on Lake	212,000 Acre-feet
minus	Evaporation from Lake	352,000 Acre-feet
equals	Outflow to Truckee River	177,000 Acre-feet

Storage Capacity of Lake Tahoe: 110,000,000 Acre-feet (35 trillion gallons), larger than the total of the four largest man-made lakes in the U.S.

U.S. Bureau of Reclamation owns water rights from elevations 6223 to 6229 feet (240 billion gallons)

Rivers and Streams flowing into Lake Tahoe, with annual flows:

Drainage	Annual Runoff	
	Acre-feet Annually	Percent of Total
Upper Truckee	60,200	19.6
Trout Creek	42,800	13.9
Taylor Creek	30,300	9.8
Blackwood Creek	19,600	6.4
Ward Creek	18,900	6.1
58 Other Creeks	171,800	55.7
Total	307,900	100.0

Outflow from Lake Tahoe into Truckee River: 177,000 Acre-feet annually

GLOSSARY

Arboretum: An area of specially planted and cared-for trees

Avalanche: A large mass of snow with included rocks and soil, which moves quickly downslope

Broadleaved tree: Trees with flattish leaves; technically, Angiosperms.

Browse: The part of the tree which animals eat.

Cambium layer: The layer of wood in a tree where cells are actively dividing; the tree cannot grow when this layer is absent or destroyed.

Catkin: A narrow, usually drooping, cluster of flowers

Chlorophyll: A green substance in leaves which is essential to production of carbohydrates by A plant

Clone: An organism with a genetic code duplicating its parent's

Compound leaf: A leaf composed of several individual leaflets occurring together in certain plants.

Cone: A woody, commonly round structure in some trees which contains and protects the tree's seeds.

Conifer: Commonly, "evergreen" trees which produce cones; technically, Gymnosperms.

Cork Cambium: The layer in which cells divide into either inner or outer bark cells

Cork Bark: The dead outer bark

dbh: The diameter of a tree at breast height (4 1/2 feet)

Deciduous: Refers to a plant which loses all of its leaves at some time each year

Earlywood: The wood formed early in the growing season

Evergreen: A plant whose leaves are green all year.

Fault: A zone of weakness in a rock along which movement takes place

Fetch: The distance across a body of water over which the wind can pile up waves

Fleur-de-lis: Literally, "the flower of the lily"; stylized to make the emblem of France; the shape of iris flowers, and an apt description of Incense Cedar cones.

Floodplain: The area surrounding a river or stream channel which becomes covered with water when the channel cannot carry all the water supplied to it

Food Factory: Another term for the leaves, which manufacture food for the plant using raw materials

Foliage: The leaves or needles of a plant.

Fungus: a plant which receives part or all of its energy from other plants rather than sunlight.

Glaciation: The geologic process by which ice shapes mountains and valleys.

Graben: block of crust which drops when the blocks on each side of it spread

Gradient: The rate of change of elevation in a river or stream channel

Heartwood: The part of the tree trunk filled with resin; this gives the tree strength to keep standing.

Inner Bark: The part of the bark through which food is transported from the leaves (=phloem)

Joint: A zone of weakness in a rock along which no movement takes place

Lake Tahoe Basin: The area inside of which all water drains into Lake Tahoe

Landslide: A downslope movement of rock, trees and soil, often rapid

Lateral Moraine: The deposit formed between a valley glacier and the valley wall

Latewood: The wood formed during summer, fall and winter

Leader: The part of a plant which grows vertically

Leaflet: A single leaf in a tree with compound leaves.

Medial moraine: A hill formed by rocks and soil scraped off mountainsides where two glaciers met; remain after glacier has melted.

Mudflow: The downhill flow of a mixture of mud, rock and water or ice

Needle: An individual leaf of a conifer tree, so named because of its long, narrow shape.

Needle Scar: The structure formed where a needle has fallen off a branch

Outer Bark: The part of the tree responsible for protection of the tree

Outwash Plain: An area covered with sediments carried downhill from a glacier by melted ice

Paper pulp: The soft wood of certain trees which is used in the manufacture of paper.

Parasite: An organism which steals it nourishment from another organism

Phloem: The part of the bark through which food is transported from the leaves (=inner bark)

Photosynthesis: The process whereby a plant converts carbon dioxide and water to carbohydrates

Riparian: Along a river or stream

Roche moutonee: A landform resulting when a glaicer moves over resitant rock

Rose hips: The part of the rose flower developed to contain seeds; sometimes used as a cosmetic.

Sapwood: The part of the tree through which are conducted fluids essential to the tree's life and growth.

Shade tolerance: The amount of low-light level a particular species of tree can tolerate and still thrive.

Species: All members of a group of orgainsims capable of interbreeding

Talus slope: A steep-angled rock pile caused when the Valley wall is attacked by frost action; frequently has few trees or shrubs.

Tap root: A vertical root sent down from the middle of the trunk in some kinds of trees to ensure a more steady supply of water.

Terminal moraine: The deposit formed when the downhill edge of a glacier stays in one spot for a period of time

Terrace: A floodplain cut into by a river after there has been uplift

Tree line: The upper elevation at which trees grow

Truckee River Basin: The area inside of which all water drains into the Truckee River

Valley Glacier: A river of ice moving down a steep mountain valley

Variety: A subgroup of a species with even more similarity between members of the subgroup

Vascular cambium: The layer of cells which divide to form either wood or bark

Volcanic neck: The opening through which volcanic material enters the earth's surface

INDEX

water use 39
Watson, Robert 42
Watson Cabin 42, 147
weddings 48
West River Road 89, 195
West Shore 22-39
wheelchairs 35, 75, 95
White Pine Blister Rust 138
Whittell, George 51, 57
Willow, Not Scouler 142, 188, 192
Willow, Scouler 32, 75, 78, 141-
    142, 149, 158-162, 189, 192
Willow, Weeping 130, 19
willows 22, 25, 32-34, 44, 79, 89,
    144, 161, 165, 189, 192 wind
Wisteria 82, 189
wood rings 12-16, 31, 142, 177
wood uses 5,11,12,30,31,45-46

Y

yard trees 98-130
Yellow Pine Belt 72
Yosemite Valley 15

Z

Zephyr Cove 60
Zolezzi Road 81
Zumwalt, J.H. 186

Wide-(eye)d Publications

P. O. Box 964   Carnelian Bay, CA 96140
(916) 546-1149   FAX (916) 546-5948

SHARE your ADVENTURES!

Now TWO great Tree Adventure books --

Order today from your choice:

_____ copies of TREE ADVENTURES AT TAHOE
(ISBN 1-885155-03-4; $9.95 plus $2.00
S & H; California residents add $0.70 tax)

_____ copies of TREE ADVENTURES IN
YOSEMITE VALLEY
(ISBN 1-885155-02-6; $7.95 plus $2.00
S & H; California residents add $0.62 tax)

NAME _____

ADDRESS _____

_____

_____

(Please send check or money order)